SpringerBriefs in Political Science

List of Figures

List of Tables

Chapter 1
Introduction

Vietnam is undergoing a process of rapid societal and economic transformation as it is moving from a centralized to an increasingly market-based economic model. As a result, Vietnam recently left its low-income status and joined the middle-income countries. It will attempt, in the future, to try to achieve high income status. This is a process through which a number of other East and Southeast Asian states have already passed.

Yet Vietnam's path must necessarily diverge from the earlier examples because of the increasing importance of multilateralism in economic decision-making, the global environmental crisis and the emergence of the fourth industrial revolution. This book explores the political economy of these changes in Vietnam from several perspectives with a view to trying to understand how such changes might be incorporated into future practice.

1.1 Political Economy

The political economy, according to Mill (1844), refers to the 'Consumption of the Community, and that Supply upon which the consumption depends.' Those aspects of consumption and supply which do not require the intervention of human labour (i.e. 'the air, the light of the sun, water') need, he thought, be included in this consideration. From this, Mill argues, it is possible to derive and examine four sets of laws: those which regulate the production of commodities; those according to which the commodities, produced by the labour of the community, are distributed; those according to which commodities are exchanged for one another and those which regulate consumption (Mill 1844). These are the issues which affect and are affected by the relationships between the individual, the state and the market. These relationships vary in place and time—that is, solutions that appear rational and obvious in one place may not appear to be so in another place and those solutions might require to be

J. Walsh et al., *The Political Economy of Vietnam's Industrial Transformation*, SpringerBriefs in Political Science,
https://doi.org/10.1007/978-981-16-0151-4_1

replaced by others as circumstances change and as the external environment changes. For example, the banking crisis of 2008 and the subsequent crisis of austerity meant that the ability of the state to conduct various operations was greatly reduced because of the money that was spent to bail out the banks and because of the diminution of tax returns afterwards. The current coronavirus pandemic is equally, perhaps even more disruptive and its effects may persist for decades to come. Further, technology makes changes to what different institutions can do: the creation of the internet meant that, among other things, it was possible for government agencies to provide services at a distance, while offering individuals the opportunity to become directly connected to either state or market agencies. Since changes are now occurring at an unprecedented rate, the nature and number of possible arrangements is so great that it is impossible for any institution to be able to determine immediately what is the most effective way to respond to any particular situation. As a result, it has become necessary increasingly to debate what should be done in response to different situations and to conduct experiments in order to collect evidence for future practice. This means that issues within political economy tend not to be determined and fixed once and for all but are subject to regular review and reconsideration.

While Mill considered that issues related to the natural environment need not be included as part of political economy, the emergence of various elements of environmental crises has made them central elements of the political economy:

> So many causes of the environmental crisis are structural, with roots in social institutions and economic relationships, that anything other than a political treatment of the environment lacks credibility (Redclift 2014:2).

The political element of the consideration relates directly to Mill's series of laws and their concern with the relationship between consumption and production. As it has become increasingly evident that the environment is infinite neither in its bounty nor its resilience, then it is necessary to consider the role of people in consuming nature and in reproducing it for the future. In the UK, for example, the production of chemicals from industrial activities led to smog which killed hundreds of people at home and acid rain which had serious impacts in Scandinavia (Barnaby 1988). Consequently, individuals and communities in the UK and Scandinavia looked to their state agencies to bring about change to market activities to protect them and their families. Owing to the regular occurrence of market imperfections with respect to negative externalities such as pollution and accident (e.g., Bhopal, Shirtwaist, Exxon Valdez), it is only through state action that appropriate responses can be found.

The environmental angle helps to make it clear that there are venues or sites where political economy contestation can take place: collective action; institutions and political market[1] imperfections (Keefer 2004). Together, these three sites represent the opportunity for multi-stakeholder interactions to take place to determine and define potential solutions to existing or emergent problems on a joint basis. This represents the situation in Vietnam today, as it is in many other countries. New problems and issues have emerged into the field of public discourse where they have

[1] 'Political market imperfections' is read as 'market and political market imperfections'.

begun to compete with the already existing wicked problems that have continued from the past to affect the present. Wicked problems are those which are "… complex, involving multiple possible causes and internal dynamics that could not be assumed to be linear and have very negative consequences for society if not addressed properly (Peters 2017)" and include inequality, drug use and environmental degradation.

It is a suitable moment, therefore, to take stock of the political economy of Vietnam, examining the different pillars of that political economy and the means by which they interact through examination of the history of the country's rapid development and is the specific issues through which the future of the country's development will take place (e.g. special economic zones and the environment). The purpose of this examination is to locate Vietnam's political economy within the spectrum of possible political economies that might exist and to try to identify possible areas of improvement.

1.2 Very Late Industrialization

Starting with Japan in the years following WWII, East Asian countries have in turn passed through processes of rapid industrial transformation. Although specific circumstances have varied, the model of development adopted has tended to have the same basic characteristics of import-substituting, export-oriented intensive manufacturing based on low labour costs. The export element of the model has been greatly facilitated by the willingness of western countries to open their markets to goods as part of the effort to restrain Communism in the Cold War period. It has also been possible for corporations of one country to benefit from wars taking place in another regional neighbour: Japanese corporations benefited from the Korean Civil War, for example, while Korean corporations subsequently profited from the Second Indochina War.

Perhaps the most notable and most studied episode of East Asian industrial transformation was that of the four Tigers of South Korea, Taiwan, Hong Kong and Singapore. In addition to pursuing a similar economic model, these states also shared in facing common existential threats affecting them at the time of transformation and which heightened the need for swift empowerment. South Korea was threatened by a resumption of hostilities in the Civil War, Hong Kong and Taiwan might have been subject to reunification attempts by China, while Singapore was facing a confrontation with Malaysia. Irrespective of the potency of the economic model that they employed; these states certainly had strong incentives to postpone immediate consumption for the sake of a better chance of survival in the long run.

Controversy has accompanied the analysis of East Asian rapid industrialisation and became particularly notable in the early 1990s, when the World Bank was leading the attempt to try to determine the critical drivers of economic growth through a series of cross-country multiple regressions, which centred on the concept of total factor productivity (TFP).[2] The controversy surrounding the analysis centred, then as now, on the role of the state in facilitating growth. It has become generally accepted that governments had a role in promoting growth through the provision of industry policy of some sort, yet the term industry policy is vague and almost all-encompassing in describing the wide range of activities that governments might pursue in seeking to enhance economic growth. It is a form of development strategy, which involves "... such wide-ranging areas as the establishment of long-term targets for growth and structural change, investments in productive facilities and infrastructure, the supply of an adequate labour force with industrial competence and discipline, and technological catching up and development (Chang 2006:100-1)."

To some extent, this can be seen, which is the line followed by the economist Krugman (1994), as primarily the result of putting to work resources which were otherwise being left unused—i.e. through unemployment or under-employment or through structural societal issues such as preventing women from entering the labour force or a caste system. This is also a variant of Kaoru Sugihara's thesis that the industrial revolution in the west was matched by the industrious revolution of the east:

> ... in the eighteenth and early nineteenth centuries China experienced an 'industrious revolution' that established a distinctive East Asian technological and institutional path. Particularly significant in this respect was the development of a labour-absorbing institutional framework centred on the household and, to a lesser extent, the village community (Arrigi 2009).

This argument is based on the need to circumvent resource constraints through the application of human labour to sustain and increase output: "The development of labour-intensive technology centring on rice cultivation enabled small-scale production labour-intensive and efficient, while the identification of the peasant family as a production unit made labour absorption easier and the incentive to work greater. It also encouraged the peasant's will to develop managerial and interpersonal skills, and anticipate and prevent potential problems. Commercialisation of agriculture and proto-industrialisation reinforced this path (Sugihara 2004)." In general, the East Asian period of rapid industrial transformation has often seen states achieve the transition from low income to medium income or medium-high income through the application of some form of the East Asian Economic Model (EAEM): import-substituting, export-oriented intensive manufacturing based on low labour cost competitiveness. However, a number of states have become stuck at that point of transformation, since they are unable to move to high income status. This is generally a result of the Middle-Income Trap (MIT): that is, the means by which it is possible to transition to middle income status are not the same means by which it is possible to transition to high income status. Malaysia and Thailand are examples of states which have not been able to reach high income status because of the unwillingness to trust the people with freedom of speech and association. In the case of Malaysia, this has been because of the threat of inter-ethnic violence that might

[2] Somewhat ironically, perhaps, a recent paper has made the claim that the search for TFP was something of a chimera, since the central variables concerned were related definitionally, thereby rendering the analysis fruitless (Felipe and McCombie 2017).

follow weakening of the state's hand on society and, in the case of Thailand, it has been because of the unwillingness of the palace-military complex to yield the power and privilege it has accumulated over the course of decades. The one state that does seem to have achieved high income status without granting personal freedoms is Singapore, yet it is argued that the balance of control, wealth and economic innovation that is possible at the limited scale of a city state is not scalable to a medium-sized state or larger. Looming on the horizon is the rival paradigm of the China model: the EAEM is reinvented with special economic zones and extensive development of physical infrastructure which has so far proved successful in marrying economic growth with the maintenance of monolithic political control. Understandably, many people in mainland Southeast Asia look at these options askance and prefer instead the example of Korea. As will be shown below, Vietnam has now passed from low income to middle income status as a result of the application of its version of the EAEM and must begin to think of means of circumventing the MIT. The issue of public administration reform, which began at the outset of the *Đổi Mới* period, is one which continues to be considerable significance in hoping to facilitate necessary changes to bring about state-level developmental goals.

1.3 Vietnam

Vietnam is the largest (310,070 km^2) and most populous (c.97 million) member of the Greater Mekong Subregion (GMS), which is a region proposed by the Asian Development Bank (ADB) to be a coherent territory for the purpose of economic development because of the long history of cultural and social congruity, together with frequent two-way border crossings of labour and capital and the sharing of some important societal institutions. The other GMS members are Cambodia, Lao PDR, Myanmar, Thailand, Yunnan Province of China and Guangxi Zhuang Autonomous Region. The ADB has begun numerous projects aimed at enhancing growth in the GMS as a whole and increasing integration among the various states within it, so as to take advantage of regional and global value chains in a period in which purely national development is no longer widely considered to be a viable approach. The most prominent of these projects is the Asian Highway Network (AHN), which aims, at considerable expense, to link by road and rail all the principal places of production and consumption not just in the GMS but the whole of Asia. Together with the signing of bilateral and multilateral free trade agreements (FTAs), the AHN has helped to transform trade and the distribution of goods regionally and led to some significant changes in the architecture of comparative and competitive advantages.

Vietnam's history with respect to transnational organizations has been very complex, owing to lengthy periods of colonisation and the struggles necessary to achieve independence. The reunification of the country at the end of the Second Indochina War (1955–75) was followed by an international economic boycott of the country led by the USA and additional fighting following the occupation of Cambodia (1975–89) and the Sino-Vietnamese War of 1979. This period of conflict was ended through peaceful negotiations and demonstrated by Vietnam's membership of international organizations: The Association of Southeast Asian Nations (ASEAN) in 1995; the Asia-Europe Meeting (ASEM) in 1996; Asia-Pacific Economic Cooperation (APEC) in 1998 and the World Trade Organization (WTO) in 2007. Despite organizations such as ASEAN maintaining the principle of non-interference in the affairs of other member nations, it is nevertheless the case that membership has brought Vietnam ever more strongly into the realm of multinational agreements and the need to subordinate, where necessary, national interest to the needs of membership. Following the end of the Cold War in 1989, Vietnam adopted the *Đổi Mới* economic strategy which was aimed at replacing the command economy, which had been in operation since 1975, with market-based mechanisms, while retaining the existing political system. This policy initially favoured stabilisation over micro-efficiency, with an early emphasis placed on agriculture (Irvin 1995) and a consistent emphasis on poverty eradication. Together with rapid and sustained growth in gross domestic product (GDP) resulting from the application of the EAEM described above (and considered further in Chaps. 4 and 5), poverty has declined significantly. According to a World Bank report from 2018, "About 70 percent of Vietnam's population can now be classified as economically secure, including the 13 percent who are now part of the global middle class (World Bank 2018:1)."

This success is attributed to a construct of three factors: boosting labour productivity and investing in infrastructure to sustain job creation and wage growth without losing competitiveness; implementing education reforms designed to equalise opportunities and develop workforce skills and spurring agricultural structural transformation through changing farmland use patterns, strengthening land use rights and improving skills of poor farmers (*ibid*.:2–3). This approach combines the government's ability to encourage human capital formation to search for opportunities that people can find for themselves. It is an approach that follows to some extent Sugihara's concept of the Asian industrious revolution, while steering a course between "… a phenomenon of either highly abstract—or 'place-less'—global market forces (the typical neoliberal approach) or of concrete national development states anchored fundamentally within Asia (the typical neo-Weberian approach (Glassman 2018:4))." This process features classes and class fractions acting: "States—autonomous or otherwise—do not act; rather classes and class fractions act through them, just as they act through markets (*ibid*.:378)." That is, the role of an active state is to provide incentives for class-defined actors to pursue the desired state-level developmental goals either because they themselves directly benefit from doing so or, else, will face penalties or disadvantages because of failing to do so. The state also has a role in its passive aspect in the same way, by encouraging a general atmosphere in which some positive aspects are immanent. The approach is similar to that identified by the economist Alfred Marshall, who observed of the proximity of the factors of production: "The mysteries of the trade become no mysteries; but as it were in the air, and children learn many of them unconsciously (Marshall 1890)."

Consequently, the relations between production and consumption, as set out in Mill's laws, are not enacted by monolithic forces but by ever-shifting coalitions of different forces and actors which act according to their own interest but which, in combination, tend to form what may be called a single class. It is argued in this book that this describes the means by which political economic change may be best understood in contemporary Vietnam.

At the same time, this very late stage of industrialization through which Vietnam is passing is the age of global environmental crisis. The evidence of manmade climate change caused by the emission of greenhouse gases into the atmosphere, together with the degradation evidenced by the presence of single-use plastic items in the remotest parts of the world and at the bottom of the Mariana Trench, as well as the imminent threat of the catastrophic loss of biodiversity have, together, brought about a situation in which it is impossible to progress in the ways that have taken place before.[3] Vietnam must face the situation in which its transformation should incorporate some means of ensuring that it is not contributing to adverse climate change above and beyond what membership of multinational organizations and the obligations that this requires. The issue of the extent to which Vietnam, as a colonised and what structural dependency theorists call a 'peripheral state' (cf. Wallerstein 1974) is responsible for causing and solving these problems is complex; currently, the best approach to a solution seems to lie in a series of multinational agreements and commitments which are, so far as is reasonably possible, sensitive to such historical issues.

At the same time that Vietnamese industrialisation is taking place in the age of global environmental catastrophe, it is also taking place in the age of a degree of contemporary technological development that is unprecedented in recorded human history. This technological change has been led by the internet and platforms and applications that use it. Combined with the establishment of finance capitalism around most of the world, the internet has (among other things, some of which are beneficial) produced a globalised society in which it appears that all imaginable goods and services have become commodified and separated, therefore, from their historical roots. To some extent, this is an inevitable result of the New International Division of Labour (NIDL),[4] which was used to demonstrate (albeit in a contested manner) that production of pretty much anything could take place pretty much anywhere. In addition, the technology has led to the introduction of the Industry 4.0 concept, which posits a fourth industrial revolution and is "… based on the digital revolution. It is characterised by a much more ubiquitous and mobile internet, by smaller and more powerful sensors that have become cheaper, and by artificial intelligence and machine learning (Schwab 2017:7)."

This revolution, if this is what it is, will have as much an impact on manufacturing and assembly as it does on every other sector of the economy and, consequently, will herald significant changes for the EAEM. Manufacturing, according to this model, will definitely by detached from the Fordist mass production model. This represents the third way, that is, in which very late Vietnamese rapid industrialisation will

[3]Recent reports show that Antarctic ice is thinning at five times the pace of the 1990 s and, in some areas, 100 m of ice thickness has melted (Carrington 2019). There are alarming reports such as this emerging on a daily basis. See also Reuters (2019) and Watts (2018).

[4]This term was developed by Frobel et al. (2009).

necessarily vary from the processes successfully passed through by other East and Southeast Asian states: the impracticality of a state being able to manage development within its own states without consultation of other interests; the presence of the global environmental crisis and the emergence of the implications of the fourth industrial revolution. The impact of these factors on the nature of changes in Vietnamese political economy in the recent past will be examined in this book, together with an assessment for how they will require changes in the foreseeable future.

1.4 The Structure of the Book

In addition to this introductory chapter, this book is organized into six subsequent chapters and then a brief conclusion. The selection of chapters has been approached as a means of trying to identify the political economic processes by which Vietnam has reached the situation in which it now finds itself and then the impact of the policies and external issues by which an attempt to move towards higher income status will be made.

Chapter 2 considers the opening of the Vietnamese economy, with an assessment of the achievements made and challenges still to be faced. The failure of the command economy and a crisis of resources which threatened the existence of the regime pushed market-based reform in the Party Congress VI (1986). Since this major milestone, Vietnam has increasingly become a trading nation after years of pursuing an export-oriented economy. It is today one of the most open economies in the world. It has been viewed as a dynamic player in the global economy with increasingly proactive participation in several deep regional trade agreements. The nation is an attractive destination for foreign investors. Its potential market has attracted many multinational companies. Several large lead firms have selected Vietnam for their production base in their global value chain due to geopolitical conditions and resources. After about three decades of transforming, by 2015, Vietnam had achieved several important Millennium Development Goals and it has become a middle-income country. Although not as successful as other East Asian countries such as Japan, South Korea or China, Vietnam's economic growth has nevertheless been relatively rapid and stable. There are, however, contemporary challenges facing the economy. The domestic enterprises do not well connect with foreign-invested enterprises, which is demonstrated in low participation and low local content of domestic enterprises in global value chains. Its main exports are labour-intensive products. The primary products are based on cheap labour and natural resource and the markets for these products are volatile due to global competition. The fast-aging population looms large and natural resources are limited, while the accumulation of capital for development has had to rely on foreign sources. Moving forward, the sustainability of economic development in Vietnam will be challenged by the adverse impact of climate change, the ineffectiveness of the public sector (including the SOEs) and the low productivity of the entire economy. The objectives of this chapter are twofold: first, to provide a background of the Opening of the Vietnamese Economy; second, to present the achievements and the challenges facing it.

Chapter 3 is related to public administration reform (PAR), with respect to both effort and achievement. The move to a market-based economy requires a reform in the public administration model which has suffered from the consequences of years of pursuing a centrally planned model. There have been several attempts aimed at PAR, especially since the early 2000s. However, there remains much to be accomplished before catching up with regional Asian peers. One of the overall objectives formally written into the 2001–2010 PAR master programme was to build a force of cadres and public servants who have appropriate capacities and ethical qualities to meet the requirements of national building and development. A review in 2010 by the parliament shows that this target was not achieved. There remains a number of steep hurdles on the path to a strong force of public service. It is not just in isolated cases that cadres and public servants have delayed their work, misbehaved with citizens or indulged in corruption. In general, the capacity of public servants, particularly in local government agencies, remains limited. There are four main reasons that explain these problems. First is the low salary of public servants. Second is the problem of patronage and nepotism. Overstaffing is the third reason. The final reason is the poor quality of public servants themselves. One direct consequence is that qualified public servants tend to leave the public sector and potential qualified candidates do not apply. However, important causes that stem from the organizing principles of the Party and State have not been discussed in sufficient detail. The argument in this chapter will centre on the organizing principles of the Party and State which constrain the advance of PAR. Particular problems in these principles are the lack of independence of the National Assembly (at national level) and People's Council (at provincial levels), opaque accountabilities of Party and State leaders (at all levels) and the constraints on central and local government leaders in exercising their authority.

Chapter 4 is related to the movement from state to market, which is one of the central issues involved in analysing political economic change. This chapter provides insights about the development of corporate governance rules in Vietnam and provides an analysis of the current challenges for regulators and firms in improving the governance mechanisms. Chief to the reforms undertaken in Vietnam since the *Đổi Mới* Policy initiated in 1986 was the creation of a "Socialist-oriented market economy." In practice, this meant the gradual injection of market mechanisms into what was previously a centrally-controlled command economy. To achieve the transition, the reforms entailed the shift from 100% government ownership to a partially privately-owned economy, starting in particular in 1992 with a "demutualization" of state-owned enterprises (SOEs) and transformation into shareholding or limited liability companies. Alongside this new form of private ownership, the government promulgated the Vietnam Enterprise Law and Securities Law in 2005, which provided the basic rules for the establishment, management and operations of these new privately-owned companies. The Enterprise Law also provided the basic principles of corporate governance mechanisms regulating the relationship between the owners and managers of privately-owned firms. These rules were a necessity for the privately-owned firms as in SOEs the owner is the manager. Now there is a large number of SOEs being transformed into shareholding companies or limited liability companies through the equitization programme. The relative newness of the corporate governance rules in Vietnam explains partly why they are still regarded as lower quality standards than peers in the region—despite a number of revisions of the Enterprise and Securities Laws. The weaknesses of the system in Vietnam has detrimental effects, among others, on securities markets' depth and behaviour, investment opportunities for individuals and savings organizations, the ability to structure an efficient pension system, FDI attractiveness and, lastly, firm performance. What will the future hold? There are encouraging signs that regulators are recognizing the need to strengthen corporate governance rules in Vietnam. The State Securities Commission is planning a serious overhaul of the Code of Corporate Governance ("hard laws") in order to align them for the Vietnamese securities markets in line with international practice. In addition, these rules are becoming increasingly supplemented by "soft laws" (codes of conduct) emanating from new institutions such as the Vietnam Institute of Directors. With the combination of stronger regulations and a more widespread adoption of codes of corporate governance conduct, Vietnam can catch up with international best practice in the medium term.

Chapter 5 is concerned with one of the principal means by which states now seek to achieve rapid industrialisation, which is through the use of special economic zones (SEZs), broadly defined. Vietnam's period of rapid economic transformation started to take place after the collapse of the Soviet Union, when the policy objective of *Đổi Mới* was introduced. This was a time when neighbouring China had already begun its period of economic openness and demonstrated that it was possible to lift hundreds of millions of people out of poverty by using the SEZ model while, at the same time, not making any concessions to political plurality. This approach intensifies the normal method of economic transformation that draws labour from the agricultural sector to the industrial one until such time as supply and demand factors are balanced and the Lewisian point is reached, which requires the state to decide whether wages should continue to increase in the relative scarcity of new labour and encouraging domestic consumption rather than the export-oriented, import-substituting intensive manufacturing that had been used up to that point. While this approach has been popular throughout the GMS and, indeed, around the developing world more generally, the Vietnamese state has used this approach more extensively and more inventively than perhaps any other. With more than 300 SEZs in a variety of different categories, Vietnam has used zones both as a form of time-limited policy experiment and devolution to local government control to an extent that has not been seen elsewhere. At the same time, considerable emphasis continues to be placed in Vietnamese society on the benefits of education and this has contributed to the popularity of Vietnamese migrant labour overseas, notably in Taiwan, where deep links have developed. These developments, together with the judicious encouragement of inward foreign direct investment in an environment tempered by extraordinary historical circumstances, have led to labour market transformation of a particularly unusual and distinctive manner, which is investigated in this chapter.

Chapter 6 is concerned with an investigation of Vietnamese political economy in East Asian and international perspectives. This chapter provides a comparative

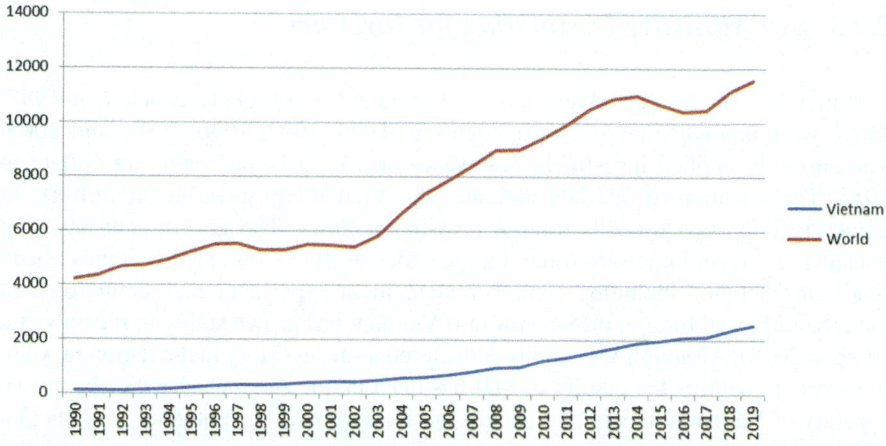

Fig. 2.2 GDP per capita of Vietnam and the World. *Source* World Bank (2020)

and the world has increased. In 1990, the gap was US$4,185, but this (Fig. 2.2) increased to US$9,030 in 2019. The main cause (of the lag) is that the process of reforms initiated in 1986 has not been sustained at a pace strong enough and boosted comprehensively, especially in institutional reforms including ownership and national governance (Truong Dinh Tuyen 2019).

In terms of achievements in poverty reduction, Vietnam is a success story. The nation takes the spotlight in the implementation of the millennium goals. The number of people escaping from poverty over the last 30 years is impressive. The poverty rate decreased from 58% in 1993 to below 6% in 2018, meaning that about 45 million people were lifted out of poverty during that period (World Bank 2020). Moreover, people's living standards have been improved significantly. Household products significantly increased, and the proportion of poor households decreased in all provinces and cities. Only in remote and mountainous areas, famine occasionally occurs due to seasonal disasters. By 2015 Vietnam has accomplished many millennium development goals, including the first three of poverty reduction, universal primary education, and gender equality and women rights. In addition, Vietnam has also achieved its goals on the prevention and control of diseases such as malaria, measles and HIV/AIDS. There have been many improvements in reproductive health goals (Goal 5) and global partnerships for sustainable development (Goal 8) (UNDP 2015).

It would be fair to conclude that in terms of poverty eradication, Vietnam made a giant leap since *Đổi Mới*.

2.2.3 An Attractive Destination for Investors

The first law on foreign investment in Vietnam was officially enacted in 1987. There were amendments and adjustments in 1990, 1992, 1996, 2000, and 2005. The currently applied investment law was issued in 2014 and came into effect in 2015. The attention to this law indicates the Vietnamese government's efforts in attracting important inwards foreign investment flows. The government has long considered this an important force that provides useful resources, which have been scarce in Vietnam, including capital, management experience and technology. In fact, the inflow of foreign investment into Vietnam has grown stably in recent years (Bishop 2018). Although Vietnam is considered a success story in the region in when it comes to quantity, the quality of FDI has been in question because the absorptive capacity of Vietnamese economy is still too weak to reap the potential benefits (Vu 2018).

By the end of 2019, Vietnam had 30,827 valid projects with a total registered capital of US$362.58 billion (Ministry of Planning and Investment of Vietnam 2020). The accumulated realized capital of FDI projects was estimated at US$211.78 billion, accounting for 58.4% of the total valid registered capital. Foreign investors have invested in 19/21 industries in the national economic sub-system, of which the processing and manufacturing sectors take the highest proportion with US$214.2 billion, accounting for 59.4% of the total investment capital, followed by real estate with US$58.4 billion (accounting for 16.1% of total investment), producing and distributing electricity and gas with US$23.65 billion (accounting for 6.5% total investment). To date, 135 countries and territories have made valid investment projects in Vietnam, of which South Korea is the leader with a total registered capital of US$67.71 billion (accounting for 18.7% of total investment capital). Japan ranked second with US$59.3 billion (capturing 16.4% of total investment capital), followed by Singapore, Taiwan, and Hong Kong. The major cities with high proportions of investment are Ho Chi Minh City with US$47.34 billion (accounting for 13.1% of total investment capital) and Binh Duong with US$34.4 billion (accounting for 9.5% of total investment capital). A further US$34.1 billion (capturing 9.4% of total investment capital) has been invested in Hanoi (Ministry of Planning and Investment of Vietnam 2020). In 2018, according to the World Investment Report (UNCTAD 2018), Vietnam was in the top 20 countries for FDI and ranked third in Southeast Asia, after Singapore and Indonesia.

In 2019, the total export turnover of companies with foreign investment reached US$181.35 billion, accounting for nearly 68,8% of Vietnam's total exports. Regarding import turnover, the foreign invested sector reached US$145.5 billion, accounting for 57.4% of national import turnover, and creating a trade surplus of US$35.86 billion (Ministry of Planning and Investment of Vietnam 2020).

One of the reasons bolstering Vietnam's rapid economic growth is the reliance on FDI. From 1986–2016, a total registered capital of about US$300 billion from 78 countries and regions was poured into Vietnam. In 2017, FDI accounted for 50% of industrial output and about 70% of Vietnam's industrial exports, and in some items such as mobile phones they account for 100% of exports. Trade balance in the country has been fuelled by the FDI sector (Malesky 2017). During 2013–2015, while domestic enterprises experienced a trade deficit every year, FDI firms exported surpluses of US$13.7 billion, US$17 billion and US$17.1 billion respectively. FDI's contribution to the total investment capital in Vietnam at 25.5% was very high compared to other countries such as China (3%), Malaysia (14.3%) and Thailand (11%) (ADB 2017).

Overall, it is worth saying that the achievements of Vietnam through decades of development need to be recognized as significant contributions for the country's further evolution. With an increasing influence in the global political economy, Vietnam is attempting to step up and integrate with global leaders systematically. More notably, the high pace of economic development promises and highlights potential attractiveness for foreign investors to come in and grow together with Vietnam as an emerging economy. Nevertheless, Vietnam is still a country with low per capita income and a modest economic size. Significant threats or challenges have been announced for the country's future development, which require further considerable efforts from both public and private sectors to overcome and make Vietnam a true influencer in the region.

2.3 Challenges

Global researchers and reporters have pointed out major hurdles on the road of Vietnam towards strong and sustainable development. In this section, the principal hurdles will be discussed to set the ground for understanding Vietnam's next steps regarding national development. First, problems associated with public management will be addressed to consider the performance of the government and signify potential gaps that need to be bridged in public work force management and efficiency of state-owned enterprises (SOEs). Second, the discussion is extended by demographic settings, which specify challenges regarding the aging population and structural unemployment. Thirdly, forces underlying the whole economy's low productivity will be investigated, which is followed by issues in the relationship with China. Finally, impacts of climate change and environment degradation are presented as one of the most significant consequences of FDI and industrialization.

2.3.1 Underperformance of the Public Sector

2.3.1.1 State-Owned Enterprise Problems

In Vietnam, SOEs make up an important part of the economy. These enterprises account for 28% of the nation's GDP (Ngoc Thuy 2019). Yet, the equitization (privatization) of SOEs in Vietnam has not been without its challenges. First, several large

SOEs have made poor investments. Inefficient management is often a cause of poor performance. Second, a lack of transparency can also be problematic. Although the government's Decree № 81/2015/NĐ-CP required some 620 SOEs to publish information, including financial and corporate governance data, at least 380 had failed to fully comply as of year-end 2016, according to the Ministry of Planning and Investment (Vietnam Plus 2018). This lack of clarity creates uncertainty concerning the true performance and fair value of SOEs. Thirdly, conflict of interest is another reason for the slow pace of privatization of Vietnamese SOEs. Incumbent executives may fear losing their positions of power within the firms after privatization, particularly when financial institutions invest and take a more active role in management (Nguyen et al. 2020).

During the period of 2000–2008, despite the ongoing privatization process, SOEs in Vietnam still received numerous forms of favourable treatment from the government. Notable cases can be found regarding credit support. Normally, Vietnam's SOEs are large in scale and can execute monopoly power in various protected industries. In addition, there have been no special laws on SOEs despite their significant impacts on the national economy, which complicates the privatization of these firms (Nguyen et al. 2020). To elaborate on credit support from the government to SOEs, it is argued that state firms do not only tend to invest more but they also benefit from higher possibilities of being funded by both commercial and subsidized institutions (Bach Thang Ngoc 2019). Consequently, there is a signal of disproportionate credit allocation across firm ownership in Vietnam. To illustrate, in 2008, the number of SOEs accounted for only 2% of the total of Vietnam's manufacturing firms. These were entitled to 15.3% of total investment, 26.8% of commercial credit and 48% of subsidized credit taken by the manufacturing sector. On the other hand, private companies in 2008 made up 84.8% of total firms in Vietnam's manufacturing sector, which took 44.9% of total investment, but only received around 38% of total commercial credit and 42.9% of total subsidized credit (Bach Thang Ngoc 2019).

2.3.2 *Public Workforce*

2.3.2.1 Issues of Accountability

Despite these changes in economic model, the model of public governance in place today is little changed from the period of the American War. As a result, there have been proposed measures from senior leaders of the state and party (Andersson et al. 2002; Da Trang 2005; Dang 2009; Shultz and Le 1993) for holding the leadership from the party and the state apparatus to be accountable, notably the following four key suggestions: (i) the National Assembly's (NA's) independence and representative capacity need to be further enhanced; (ii) government leaders should be given more power to manage their allocated activities better; (iii) individual responsibility and accountability of the Party leadership should be more transparent and (iv) election of the Party General Secretary should be implemented at the party Congress. That these changes in governance have been proposed by former and current senior office holders suggests a lively concern to improve both effectiveness and accountability within the key institutions of the State.

Vietnam suffers from entrenched corruption, especially in SOEs (Kolko 2001; Turner et al. 2017), Transparency International (2019) ranks Vietnam as 96th in its global perception of corruption index. The resolution of the 3rd Party Central Committee Plenum in 2007 acknowledged corruption as a threat to the Party and the regime: The fight against corruption and waste remains ineffective (Party General Secretary 2007). Corruption and waste are serious and occurring in many industries, many levels and many areas at large scale, resulting in severe consequences. This practice affects people's trust and thus that is one of the most dangerous threats to the Party and the regime.

There have been several corruption scandals which indicate that the corruption has not been curbed. Others believe that the impact of the government's attempts to combat corruption is very limited and that the situation is getting worse (Fforde 2009). "Hot on the top, cold at the bottom" was the phrase used by General Secretary Nguyen Phu Trong when talking about the situation of slow change at grass-root levels at local governments while there was determination from the central level (Bao Tran 2018). Local authorities tend to wait for the signal from the central government before taking initiatives (Nguyen Quoc Suu 2018). Vietnam has dropped its ranking in Corruption Perception Index, from 107th in 2017 to 117th in 2018. Although there was an improvement in the 2019 ranking, corruption in Vietnam is still rampant according to this ranking.

Political experts believe that the reason why many subordinates are indifferent towards the work of Party building and anti-corruption stems from insufficient awareness, which is said to be led by the fact that authorities at lower levels have not fully grasped the Central Resolution. The organization and efforts of learning and adapted Resolutions from the Central Government tend to be mere formality, which means Party members are not fully aware of the urgency of the Party's construction and adjustment. Additionally, further possible reasons can range from the subjective awareness of officers, party organizations and authorities to the bureaucratic, cumbersome and inefficient administrative apparatus, laws and discipline. As a result, the phenomenon of "cold", originating from different causes, must be made clear before it can be overcome (Nguyen Minh 2018).

2.3.3 *Aging Population and Structural Unemployment*

2.3.3.1 An Aging Population

According to Stolnitz (2017), the demographic transition of a country has four stages. In the early stages, the birth rate is high but so is the death rate, so the population is stable or increases at a relatively low pace. In the second stage, the death rate decreases but the birth rate continues to be high, so the population increases rapidly. The characteristic of this period is that the percentage of young people (under 15 years old) is high. At the third stage, the birth rate decreases and so the population increases only slightly. The number of people born in the previous stage now becomes the labour force. During this period, the proportion of people of working age (15–65 years) is high while the proportion of the dependent population is low because there are fewer young people in the population (0–14 years), and the proportion of elder people (over 65) is not so high. This is an ideal period for economic development, known as the demographic gift or demographic bonus. It can also be called a golden population structure (Bussolo et al. 2018; Stolnitz 2017). By the fourth stage, the golden population is over and the country enters the aging population period in which the proportion of the elderly (over 65) increases. At this time, the proportion of people in working age decreases and the number of dependent people is large, so the burden of social welfare is on the shoulders of people of working age (Stolnitz 2017). Owing to the importance of changes in the population structure, the best development path of a country is from the second phase to prepare the prerequisites for strong development in the third phase, for example, by quickly universalizing basic education and building infrastructure (Lehfeldt 2017).

The proportion of the Vietnamese population in the working age began to increase in 1970 (about 51%), peaking at 71% in 2020. Consequently, it can be said that the period of the golden population in Vietnam was from about 1970 to 2020 (Tran Van Tho 2015). This means Vietnam is about to exit the period of golden population. Compared to other developed countries, the aging rate in Vietnam is relatively higher and ranks among the world's highest (Mai Dan 2019). In developed countries, the transition from golden population or demographic dividend to aging population can take decades or even centuries. For example, France took 115 years, Australia took 73 years and China took 26 years, while Vietnam is forecasted to take only 15 years (Ha-An 2019). Furthermore, Ōizumi (2013) investigated the time it takes to double the population aging rate, from 7% (an aging nation) to 14% (an aged nation), to come up with a primary indicator for the pace of population aging amongst Asian countries as demonstrated in the following Table 2.4.

As shown above, Vietnam is scheduled to encounter the shortest transition from an aging nation to an aged nation.

An aging population is, therefore, just around the corner, which challenges the country's capability to cater for emerging needs healthcare, pharmaceuticals and education (GOV-UK 2015). As Tran Van Tho (2015, p. 46) observed "Vietnam is facing a huge challenge, which is represented by the fact that Vietnam will get old before it gets rich".

2.3.3.2 Structural Unemployment

Although Vietnam is in the final phase of enjoying the demographic dividend from the golden age structure, the problem of structural unemployment has still emerged as a hurdle for the country's national development agenda. Structural unemployment is directly linked to the shortage of skilled labour in Vietnam (Maruichi and Abe

Table 2.4 Doubling Period of Population Aging. *Source* Adapted from Ōizumi (2013), United Nations (2013)

Countries	Rate of 7%	Rate of 14%	Doubling period (years)
Japan	1970	1995	25
Korea	1999	2018	19
Taiwan	1994	2017	23
Hong Kong	1984	2013	29
Singapore	1999	2021	22
China	2001	2027	26
Thailand	2002	2022	20
Malaysia	2021	2045	24
Indonesia	2023	2045	22
Philippines	2035	2075	35
Vietnam	**2016**	**2033**	**17**

2019). To provide rationales for the linkage, it is essential to investigate the notion behind structural unemployment. According to Restrepo (2015), structural unemployment refers to the type of involuntary unemployment which is mainly caused by the mismatch between the skills that workers in the labour market can offer and the skills demanded by employers. In the case of Vietnam, the labour force does not sufficiently provide the expected level of skills and knowledge to perform tasks associated with the modern developing business environment, which leads to the fact that a considerable proportion of people in the working force are not employed (Maruichi and Abe 2019). This can be one of the most problematic hurdles for the development of Vietnam in the years to come. Wendy and Obert (2018) contend that a shift in trade and consumption patterns and the rise of the global knowledge economy may provide new high-value jobs but will require a different skill set than the one Vietnam currently uses.

Skilled labour is expected to contribute to firm growth through the ability to generate new knowledge, develop innovative initiatives, capture emerging business opportunities and transfer knowledge to their co-workers (World Bank 2013). However, owing to the low quality of tertiary education, more graduates are shifting to work in secondary level jobs, despite a high demand for skilled labour in upper-level job positions (APEC Human Resource Development Working Group 2017). The structural unemployment which is fuelled by the shortage of skills has been a contributing factor to the low productivity of the whole economy of Vietnam. This issue will be discussed in the following section.

2.3.3.3 Low Productivity of the Entire Economy

In 2017, Vietnam was ranked amongst countries with the lowest labour productivity (output per worker) in Asia, in spite of showing some growth. Labour productivity of

Vietnam in 2018 was only higher than Cambodia in South East Asia, only 7.3% of the productivity of Singapore, 19% of Malaysia, 37% of Thailand, 44.8% of Indonesia and 55.9% of the labour productivity of the Philippines (Quynh Trang 2019). In 2018, while having managed to outperform Bangladesh, the manufacturing labour productivity of Vietnam remained approximately a quarter of that of China and Malaysia, a half of India and Thailand and just around 7% of that of Japan (UNDP 2019).

Vietnam has witnessed short-falls in labour productivity since the 1990s in areas such as mining, finance, real estate and other industrial subsectors. However, in agriculture, labour productivity has grown strongly but the level is still lower than other middle-income countries in the region (World Bank 2016). Other studies have confirmed that labour productivity can be measured by taking the national output divided by the number of workers (McCullough 2015). This can be modified in the case of Vietnam, as shown below.

2.3.3.4 Sizable Labour Force in Agricultural Activities

Although the number of employed labourers in agriculture, forestry and fisheries has decreased from 22.3 million in 2016 to just under 19 million in 2019, the proportion of this workforce in Vietnam still accounts for the largest proportion of the national labour structure, with almost half of the country's total workforce (Das 2018; World Bank 2016). According to the labour force survey of the Vietnam government in 2019, 66.9% of the country's labour force reside in rural areas (Le Anh 2020) and this partially explains the high proportion of agricultural labourers in Vietnam (Das 2018).

The average annual GDP growth rate of Vietnam from 1986 to 2019 was 6.5%. However, Vietnam was still categorized in the group of lower-middle-income countries by the World Bank and MPI (2016). The country is likely to fall in the middle-income trap. It is suggested that Vietnam's economy should shift from low productivity sectors, typically agricultural activities, to higher-productivity and labour-intensive manufacturing (Kikuchi et al. 2018). According to the GSO (2020), in Vietnam, agricultural activities only account for 13.9% of GDP but they facilitate the livings of nearly 67% of the population. Moreover, despite the fact that agriculture generates only half the amount of GDP that the industrial sector does, twice as many labourers are employed in agriculture compared to industry (GSO 2020). As a result, average productivity of labourers in agriculture is much lower than that of workers in industry, which leads to the low productivity of the overall economy.

2.3.3.5 Less Developed Technological Application in Production

Another explanatory factor for Vietnam's low labour productivity is backwardness in technological adoption. Despite many efforts and initiatives, Vietnam was still 50

Table 2.5 ICOR Coefficients in Vietnam. *Source* CIEM (2019)

Year	2011	2012	2013	2014	2015	2016	2017
The whole economy	5.72	6.76	6.67	6.29	5.80	6.42	6.11
Public sector	9.03	8.00	10.02	12.12	9.17	9.75	12.62

to 100 years behind in the race of technology with the world's most modern countries in 2016 (VnExpress 2016). As wages have gradually increased, the traditional comparative advantage of Vietnam in terms of cheap low-skill and labour-intensive manufacturing sectors is dissipating. This represents an urgent need for both public and private businesses to consider adopting emerging labour-saving technologies and automation in production (Eckardt et al. 2018).

In Vietnam, as discussed earlier, FDI represents a large proportion of the economy. However, the quality of many projects remains low, with little impact on economic and technological restructuring (Newman and Narciso 2009). In other words, the vertical linkages between FDI and domestic enterprises is weak, so the spill-over effect of technology and business knowledge to the economy is also weak. Large-scale FDI projects are still largely involved in assembly rather than manufacturing (Le and Pomfret 2011). Additionally, domestic supporting industries are developing slowly, so they continue to import components and other intermediate products (Tran Van Tho 2015).

2.3.3.6 Low Productivity in the Public Sector

The state-owned economic sector accounts for a significant share of the country's assets, many investment projects worth tens of trillions of VND are incurring constant losses and are now waiting for the decision whether to liquidate or continue operating. The following table calculates the ICOR coefficients of the whole economy and the state sector 2011 to 2017. ICOR is the ratio of investment to growth, measuring the marginal output of capital (Li 2016). The larger the coefficient, the less effective the investment is (Table 2.5).

The Table 2.5 shows that the ICOR coefficient has increased rapidly in recent years. In 2017, the coefficient for public economic sector was more than double of the whole economy. This once again illustrate the seriousness of the productivity in the public sector.

2.3.3.7 Poor Linkage of the Local Suppliers and Lead Firms

Despite boasting success of having FDI enterprises cultivating the economy, Vietnam has not been able to make the foreign investment flows deep-rooted and connected organically to local businesses. Like other nations in Asia, small and medium-sized enterprises (SMEs) are the predominant type of enterprise in Vietnam. According to the World Bank (2017), 97.6% of domestic enterprises are SMEs. However, as of 2017, only 21% of Vietnamese SMEs were linked with global value chains (GVCs), much lower than 30% in Thailand and 46% in Malaysia. The localization rate of Japanese enterprises in Vietnam only reached 34%, while that figure was 68% in China and 57% in Thailand (ADB 2017). Consequently, not only were foreign businesses facing higher manufacturing costs but Vietnamese enterprises were unable to reap benefits supplied for them.

Vietnam's FDI attractiveness still faces challenges in many areas. FDI has not really taken root, created spill-over and formed highly competitive industry clusters as might have been hoped. In the context that domestic enterprises have not really established a strong foothold in the international market, Vietnam's economy depends on the FDI sector (Nguyen et al. 2020). This fact aligns with findings from the study of Ignatenko et al. (2019), which observed that participation in GVCs benefits upper middle and high-income countries, while such robust benefits cannot be found in low and lower-middle income countries. To illustrate, Vietnam's garment and footwear industry is mainly engaged in processing and lacks close association with FDI enterprises in the domestic economy. There seems to be a challenging path ahead for firms in Vietnam, especially the SMEs, to upgrade in GVCs (Nguyen et al. 2020).

In Asia, SMEs also play a huge role in national economic development, representing over 95% of private enterprises (Abe et al. 2015). In Japan, until recently, a surprising 87% of all enterprises had no more than fiveworkers (Government of Japan, Ministry of the Economy and Trade and Industry 2015). Over 99% of enterprises in Thailand are SME (OSMEP 2015). Across Asia, SMEs employed about 60%–90% of the total workforce, generated 30%–70% of output and contributed 15%–40% of exports (Abe et al. 2015). However, SMEs are still underdeveloped and unequal in participating in GVCs in many parts of the world. In the Association of Southeast Asian Nations (ASEAN), the production network is still dominated by large firms. Despite being the majority of all enterprises and achieving large domestic employment generation, SMEs are still underrepresented in international trade, accounting for only 23% of ASEAN's exports (World Bank 2017). In addition, there is an imbalance in SME participation rates in GVCs between more developed countries and lesser ones. For instance, Thai and Malaysian SMEs have 30% and 46.2% GVC integration respectively, whereas SME participation rate in others are much lower: 21.4% in Vietnam, 20.1% in the Philippines and only 6.3% in Indonesia (OECD 2015). SMEs in Vietnam are facing several problems in joining and moving up the GVCs (Nguyen et al. 2020).

2.3.4 Dealing with China

China has always been the bigger player compared to Vietnam in the long-established bilateral relationship between the two countries. This section investigates the current interactions between Vietnam and China in terms of trade and politics in the context of intense East Sea conflict and the Trade War between China and the US.

2.3.4.1 Trade Deficit and Chinese Contractors in Vietnam

Over the past decade, Vietnam's international trade has been characterised by consistent and serious deficits with China (Ngoc Hoang 2020). In 2013–2017, Vietnam spent about $250 billion on importing goods from China, which is more than 200% of Vietnam's exports there (Nguyen Tuyen 2018). Vietnam's goods shipments to China face difficulties earning a profit because the Chinese currency has been devalued sharply, especially due to the on-going Trade War with the US (The Saigon Times 2019). The side effect of China's action in depreciating its currency on Vietnam's economy is significant as Chinese products will become more competitive in terms of price compared to Vietnamese ones (Tung Nguyen 2019). Additionally, there is not much room for the Vietnamese government to modify the domestic currency rate to cope with this depreciation as the country is now on the monitoring list of the US which specifies restrictions in exchange rate intervention by monetary policy, together with Japan, Korea, Germany, Italy, Ireland, Singapore and Malaysia as trade partners of the US (US Department of the Treasury 2019).

Another concern in the relationship is that Chinese overseas development assistance (ODA) tends to cost more and Chinese contractors do not deliver guaranteed quality for projects in Vietnam (Anh-Minh 2018). It has been found that the interest rate for Chinese ODA loans is nearly 3% per year, compared to 0.4–1.2% for Japanese ODA and around 1.75% for India and European Union countries. Moreover, projects using Chinese loans and Chinese contractors in Vietnam are more likely to fall behind schedule and end up with extra costs with non-guaranteed quality (Anh-Minh 2018). Significant evidence can be found in the cases of Cat Linh–Ha Dong Metro and Bauxite Tan Rai-Nhan Co (Mai Dang 2019; Xuan Nguyen 2019). Notably, Cat Linh–Ha Dong Metro has recently received tremendous attention from Vietnamese reporters. Despite its modest length of only 13 km, Cat Linh–Ha Dong Metro is recognized as one of the most time-consuming projects in Vietnam. Having conducted a prefeasibility study in 2002–2003 with financial support from Chinese ODA loans according to the framework agreement between Vietnam and China signed in 2008, there has still not been any formal announcement of the date when this project may be put officially into operation (Bich Diep 2019). The major causes for delay are on Chinese contractor's side and are associated with the contractor's low capability and the process of supplying essential equipment. This has led to doubts about the Chinese contractor's ability to ensure quality and safety standards (Le et al. 2019).

2.3.4.2 Marine Time Confrontation and Future Consequences

The growing tension in the East Sea of Vietnam has been a hot topic recently when considering the relationship between China and countries in South East Asia. The East Sea contains one of the world's busiest shipping routes with great potential for oil and gas reserves. China has attempted to claim almost all the sea area using the nine-dash line supported by military force and has been accused by the US of reaching too far in militarizing the area. Other countries alongside the US have shown concern about the activities of China in the East Sea as one of the most dangerous flashpoints in the world (Kim 2015). Looking into a recent event in South China Sea as an example helps see how aggressively China is forcing its claim over the disputed sea area. In June 2019, a Chinese vessel was found to have been involved in the ramming and sinking of a Filipino Boat, which led to 22 fishermen being lost overboard before being rescued by a Vietnamese boat (Gutierrez and Beech 2019). A spokesperson from Beijing perceived this as an ordinary maritime traffic accident and refused to talk about the Chinese vessel's responsibility. On the other side, Delfin Lorenzana, the Defense Seretary of the Philippines, believes that the crash was intentional and not an expected action from friendly and responsible people (Robles 2019). Furthermore, it is also reported that Chinese Coast Guard ships have been significantly involved in fishing activities in disputed waters by maintaining a discreet distance with Chinese fishing boats under their protection.

It is believed that if a full-blown conflict in the East Sea did happen, the first shots would be fired between China and Vietnam (Hutt 2019). In July 2019, Haiyang Dizhi 8, a Chinese survey ship with armed escort, spent weeks near the Vanguard Bank, a maritime area belonging to Vietnam's exclusive economic zone. Beijing is ramping up its aggression against Hanoi to pressurize it to terminate the exploration for oil and gas in the contested area (Zhou 2019). Chinese President Xi Jinping is confident in the People's Liberation Army (PLA) as one of the world's largest and most well-equipped military forces, which shows the country's readiness and preparation for a large-scale fight (Hutt 2019). However, China's military moves in disputed areas are challenged by the US Navy's conducting of six freedom-of-navigation operations, which are intended to examine excessive maritime claims in the Paracel Islands, Spratly Islands and other areas in the South and East China Seas.

The possibly long-lasting conflict between China and Vietnam in the East Sea creates potential disputes in the bilateral relationship, which might further hinder collaboration in economic development (Fook and Hop 2019).

2.3.4.3 Trade War Crossfire

The US is considered Vietnam's largest export market, while China is the country's largest import market. As a result, the Trade War between China and the US has many impacts on the economy of Vietnam, both positive and negative. Under the trade tensions, several global companies have shifted their production lines to Vietnam, which has benefited the country's economic development. However, it is suggested by experts that Vietnamese exporters should be cautious in preventing fraudulent rebadged signs of origins of exported goods, such as wood and seafood, to avoid being hit with US tariffs (Mai et al. 2019). There is, therefore, an urgent need for establishing a clear standard and definition for locally made goods with the "made in Vietnam" label. In fact, products made with imported material from China with slight changes do not qualify as being of Vietnamese origin. Consequently, these products will be treated as of Chinese origin in the US market (Dat Nguyen 2019).

Vietnam is considered to be able to replace China in exporting some products to the US. World media reports have also said that Vietnam benefited from this war. However, reality does not seem to show that this is an accurate observation. Take the textile industry as an example, where the US is a market that Vietnamese enterprises share with Chinese enterprises (the US imports 40% from China and 15% from Vietnam). The latest imposition of US$267 billion in consumer good tariffs such as textiles and mobile phones has created opportunities for Vietnam to increase its exports, although most of those exports are from foreign-invested enterprises (VnEconomy 2019).

In the long run, the consequences of this war on Vietnam will be considerable. The biggest negative effect is the competition with Chinese goods in non-US markets. When the Yuan decreases, Chinese goods in other markets will be cheaper and will compete directly with Vietnamese goods and, further when this happens, many inferior or surplus products from China will be pushed to Vietnam. In general, Vietnam becomes a place of consuming poor-quality goods from China. This increases the risk that Vietnam will be taxed by the US and the US President has warned Vietnam about this issue as Vietnam's trade surplus has widened (VnEconomy 2019). Notably, the trade sentiments of Trump were not only directed at China but also at any country that establishes a sizable trade surplus with the US. Recently, Trump called Vietnam "the single worst abuser of everybody" to criticize Vietnam for its initiatives to allow Chinese companies to reroute their exported products to the US (Lei 2019). Consequently, Vietnam should be wise in balancing the concerns of both China and the US to avoid the effect of crossfire during the trade war.

2.3.5 Adverse Impact of Climate Change

Within the report of Intergovernmental Panel on Climate Change (IPCC) in 2018, Vietnam was named in the group of nine countries who have at least 50 million people who will be exposed to the risk rising sea levels, abnormal climate events, storms and other dangers generated by climate change (Tatarski 2018).

The country's geography makes it more vulnerable to various calamities. The 1,800-mile-long coastline facing the East Sea exposes Vietnam to huge threats from numerous tropical storms every year. The far-north mountainous areas are prone to flash flooding and landslides and the flat Mekong Delta is named as one of the world's most vulnerable regions to rising sea levels (IPCC 2018). There have been many reports on the urgency of rising sea levels in Vietnam's Mekong Delta. According to Werner and Simmons (2009), it is estimated that a one-metre sea-level rise will flood the homes of over 14.2 million residents there. This creates pressure for the government to ensure health, well-being and safety for people living in this area in case of the future possible relocation of settlements. In a recent study of scientists from the Netherlands, it was found that the Mekong Delta is only 0.8 metres higher than sea level, which signifies a threat to the resettlement of more than 12 million residents in the next 50 years (Phuc Long 2019).

Facing significant threats from climate change, Vietnam has initiated international commitments to cope with it. Remarkably, a plan for the implementation of the Paris Climate Change Agreement has been issued by the government which focuses on promoting connections with partners, the scientific community and leading enterprises in responding to climate change (IPCC 2018).

Apart from the effects of global climate change, it is also worth noting that the environment of Vietnam has been gradually damaged by production activities of both domestic and foreign-owned firms. Adverse impacts on the local environment by FDI inflows such as dumped water, toxic gases and industrial waste have deteriorated the environment of several provinces and cities in Vietnam. According to data from the GSO (2017), Vietnam's environmental regulations have been breached by 80% of the country's industrial parks. Notably, 60% of the regulation breaching cases involve FDI companies (Ward 2019). Regarding the adverse impacts from FDI, the well-known case studies of Formosa and the Thi Vai River have been widely used as evidence for negative impacts on the local environment. Formosa Plastics took responsibility for discharging toxic waste into surrounding water, which resulted in the death of 70 tons of fish, while Vedan Vietnam admitted to the 105,600 cubic metres of untreated water dumped into Thi Vai River in 2008 (Tri et al. 2017; VietnamNet 2019).

2.4 Conclusion

This chapter has highlighted key achievements of Vietnam from the period of economic reform until now. Overall, Vietnam has realized an excellent rate of economic development. Although the country is still in the group of low and middle-low income nations, great efforts taken by the government and business sectors have increased the country's level of influence in the regional and global political economy. This is represented by important FTAs and partnerships with highly influential institutions. The discussed achievements are said to contribute strongly to the attractiveness of Vietnam for foreign investors with evidence from the continually increasing amount of accumulated FDI.

On the other hand, there are still major challenges that Vietnam needs to overcome in order to achieve further strong and sustainable development. Firstly, the ineffectiveness and inefficiency of public management have not gained any significant improvements despite strong efforts and dedication from the government. There are still gaps that need to be bridged in public workforce utilization and the management of SOEs. Secondly, Vietnam only has a few years left before the time of the golden population structure is over. It appears that the country has missed this great opportunity to take advantage of the population structure. To be more specific, despite having enjoyed the demographic benefits from the golden population structure, the structural unemployment rate is still considerable, which implies inefficiency in labour force utilization. Furthermore, low productivity and poor linkage of local suppliers and lead enterprises have led to the waste of resources and opportunities. Additionally, as one of the emerging challenges in diplomatic relation, Vietnam faces challenges stemming from the recent dispute in the East Sea of Vietnam. China is putting aggressive efforts in claiming its sovereignty over the exclusive economic zones of many countries in the region. This issue is said to be leading to a deterioration in the relationship between Vietnam and China. Moreover, current problems associated with Chinese contractors of infrastructure projects in Vietnam require a certain amount of attention from the government. The ongoing trade war between China and the US is said to bring several crossfire effects, which means Vietnam should modify its foreign policy wisely to benefit the most and avoid the negative impacts from the war. As for the final challenge of sustainable development, the adverse impact of climate change that has resulted from industrialization has significant negative potential impacts on the standards of living of Vietnamese people in the future.

Acknowledgements The authors would like to thank Nguyen Le Hoang Long and Tran Pham Khanh Toan for their research assistance.

References

Abe M, Troilo M, Batsaikhan O (2015) Financing small and medium enterprises in Asia and the Pacific. J Entrepreneurship Public Policy 4(1):2–32

ADB (2017) ASEAN Corporate Governance Scorecard Country Reports and Assessments 2015. https://www.adb.org/sites/default/files/publication/375481/asean-cgscorecard-2015.pdf

AmCham Vietnam (2014) Samsung searches for Vietnam suppliers. http://www.amchamvietnam.com/samsung-searches-for-vietnam-suppliers-without-success/

AmCham Vietnam (2019) Private sector as key driver for 2019. https://www.amchamvietnam.com/private-sector-a-key-driver-for-2019/

Andersson G, Granstedt P, Rönnmo B, Nguyen T (2002) Strengthening the capacity of the Office of the Vietnam National Assembly. Sida Evaluation 2:12

Anh-Minh (2018) Vietnam frets over Chinese ODA, contractors. https://e.vnexpress.net/news/business/vietnam-frets-over-chinese-oda-contractors-3792908.html

APEC Human Resource Development Working Group (2017) Data science and analytics skills shortage: equipping the APEC workforce with the competencies demanded by employers. https://www.apec.org/-/media/APEC/Publications/2017/11/Data-Science-and-Analytics-Skills-Shortage/217_HRD_Data-Science-and-Analytics-Skills-Shortage.pdf

Asia Regional Integration Center (2020) Free trade agreements. https://aric.adb.org/database/fta

Bach Thang Ngoc (2019) State owned enterprises and capital misallocation in Vietnam. J Asia Pacific Economy, 1–21

Bao Tran (2018) Tổng bí thư: Vẫn còn tình trạng "trên nóng, dưới lạnh". https://nld.com.vn/thoi-su/van-con-tinh-trang-tren-nong-duoi-lanh-20180410225407 82.htm

Beresford M (2008) Doi Moi in review: the challenges of building market socialism in Vietnam. J Contemporary Asia 38(2):221–243

Bich Diep (2019) Trách nhiệm chưa ai nhận, nhưng hậu quả người dân đã "lãnh đủ". https://dantri.com.vn/blog/trach-nhiem-chua-ai-nhan-nhung-hau-qua-nguoi-dan-da-lanh-du-20190924013647004.htm

Bishop B (2018) Liberalising foreign direct investment policies in the APEC region. Routledge, Abingdon

Bussolo M, Koettl J, Sinnott E (2018) Golden aging: Prospects for healthy, active, and prosperous aging in Europe and Central Asia. Public Sector Economics 3, 42(3):347–351

CIEM (2019) Kinh tế nhà nước, cơ cấu lại DNNN: Đánh giá kết quả thực hiện giai đoạn 2011–2020 và đề xuất phương hướng giải pháp cho giai đoạn 2021–2030. http://www.ciem.org.vn/tin-tuc/6585/moi-tham-du-hoi-thao-cong-bo-ket-qua-nghien-cuu-kinh-te-nha-nuoc-va-co-cau-lai-dnnn-danh-gia-ket-qua-thuc-hien-giai-doan-2011-2020-va-de-xuat-phuong-huong-giai-phap-cho-giai-doan-2021-2030

Da Trang (2005) Former Party General Secretary: anti-corruption: tneed to look to yourself. http://tuoitre.vn/Chinh-tri-Xa-hoi/80301/Chong-tham-nhung-phai-tu-xem-lai-ban-than-minh.html

Phong D (2008) Tư duy kinh tế Việt Nam – Chặng đường gian nan và ngoạn mục 1975-1989. NXB Tri Thức, Hanoi

Dang VH (2009) Unification—enhance ruling efficiency. http://www.tienphong.vn/Tianyon/Index.aspx?ArticleID=155203&ChannelID=2

Das K (2018) Labor market trends in Vietnam. https://www.vietnam-briefing.com/news/labor-market-trends-vietnam.html/

Dat Nguyen (2019) Vietnam takes steps to avoid trade war crossfire. https://e.vnexpress.net/news/business/economy/vietnam-takes-steps-to-avoid-trade-war-crossfire-3965243.html

Dinh BP (2018) Case study 8: Redefining reality: A case study of the emerging leadership of Truong Chinh. In Knowledge Creation in Public Administrations (pp. 191–210): New York, NY: Springer

Eckardt S, Mishra D, Dinh VT (2018) Vietnam's manufacturing miracle: Lessons for developing countries. https://www.brookings.edu/blog/future-development/2018/04/17/vietnams-manufacturing-miracle-lessons-for-developing-countries/

Fforde A (2009) Luck, policy or something else entirely? Vietnam's economic performance in 2009 and prospects for 2010. J Current Southeast Asian Affairs 28(4):71–94

Fforde A (2019) From 'constructing socialism'to a 'socialist-oriented market economy'in contemporary Vietnam: a critique of ideologies. Europe-Asia Stud 71(4):671–697

Fook LL, Hop HH (2019) Can Beijing and Hanoi overcome their latest South China Sea flashpoint at Vanguard Bank? https://www.scmp.com/week-asia/politics/article/3025882/can-beijing-and-hanoi-overcome-their-latest-south-china-sea

Government of Japan, Ministry of the Economy, & Trade and Industry. (2015) 2015 White Paper on small enterprises in Japan: Take-off time for micro businesses. www.chusho.meti.go.jp/pamflet/hakusyo/H27/h27/shoukibodeta/download/2015shohaku_eng.pdf

GOV-UK (2015) Vietnam: from golden age to golden oldies. Research and analysis. https://www.gov.uk/government/publications/vietnam-from-golden-age-to-golden-oldies/vietnam-from-golden-age-to-golden-oldies

GSO (2020) Tình hình kinh tế - xã hội Quý IV và năm 2020. https://www.gso.gov.vn/default.aspx?tabid=621&ItemID=19454

Gutierrez J, Beech H (2019) Sinking of Philippine boat puts South China Sea back at issue. https://www.nytimes.com/2019/06/13/world/asia/south-china-sea-philippines.html

Ha-An (2019) Vietnam population to enter super-aging phase in 2038. http://www.hanoitimes.vn/social-affair/2019/07/81e0d9c3/vietnam-population-to-enter-super-aging-phase-in-2038/

Hai Loc (2019) Điều gì níu giữ mô hình Xô Viết trong quản trị quốc gia? https://vietnamnet.vn/vn/tuanvietnam/tieudiem/dieu-gi-niu-giu-mo-hinh-xo-viet-trong-quan-tri-quoc-gia-528916.html

Herr H, Schweisshelm E, Truong MV (2016) The integration of Vietnam in the global economy and its effects for Vietnamese economic development. https://www.global-labour-university.org/fileadmin/GLU_Working_Papers/GLU_WP_No.44.pdf

Hoang Vuong Q, Napier N (2014) Resource curse or destructive creation in transition: Evidence from Vietnam's corporate sector. Management Research Review 37(7):642–657

Hutt D (2019) Why China is picking a fight with Vietnam. https://asiatimes.com/2019/09/why-china-is-picking-a-fight-with-vietnam/

Ignatenko A, Raei F, Mircheva B (2019) Global value chains: What are the benefits and why do countries participate? https://www.imf.org/-/media/Files/Publications/WP/2019/wp1918.ashx

IPCC (2018) IPCC presents findings of the Special Report on Global Warming of 1.5 °C at event to discuss Viet Nam's response to climate change. https://www.ipcc.ch/2018/10/10/ipcc-presents-findings-of-the-special-report-on-global-warming-of-1-5c-at-event-to-discuss-viet-nams-response-to-climate-change/

Kikuchi T, Yanagida K, Vo H (2018) The effects of Mega-Regional Trade Agreements on Vietnam. J Asian Econ 55:4–19. https://doi.org/10.1016/j.asieco.2017.12.005

Kim J (2015) Territorial disputes in the South China Sea: implications for security in Asia and beyond. Strategic Stud Quart 9(2):107–141

Kolko G (2001) China and Vietnam on the road to the market. J Contemp Asia 31(4):431–440

Le Anh (2020) Reviewing the employment and employment situation in 2019. http://dangcongsan.vn/xa-hoi/nhin-lai-tinh-hinh-lao-dong-va-viec-lam-2019-548623.html

Le Kien, Dung TB (2019) Bộ trưởng Nguyễn Văn Thể: Tổng thầu Trung Quốc thiếu kinh nghiệm vận hành. https://tuoitre.vn/bo-truong-nguyen-van-the-tong-thau-trung-quoc-thieu-kinh-nghiem-van-hanh-20190605084505455.htm

Le HQ, Pomfret R (2011) Technology spillovers from foreign direct investment in Vietnam: horizontal or vertical spillovers? J Asia Pac Econ 16(2):183–201

Lehfeldt EA (2017) Religious women in golden age Spain: the permeable cloister: Abingdon: Routledge

Lei A (2019) Is Southeast Asia winning the US-China trade war? Not so fast. https://thediplomat.com/2019/09/is-southeast-asia-winning-the-us-china-trade-war-not-so-fast/

Li C-G (2016) Use ICOR, DEA and Malmquist index to study on investment efficiency of urbanization of Sichuan Province, China. J Discrete Math Sci Cryptogr 19(3):801–809

Mai Dan (2019) Vietnam's population aging rate is among the fastest in the world. http://thoibaotaichinhvietnam.vn/pages/xa-hoi/2019-01-17/toc-do-gia-hoa-dan-so-cua-viet-nam-thuoc-nhom-nhanh-nhat-the-gioi-66800.aspx

Mai Dang (2019) China bans SOEs from bidding in Vietnam: No effect on projects! Nguoi Dong Hanh. https://ndh.vn/thoi-su/trung-quoc-cam-cac-dnnn-au-thau-tai-viet-nam-khong-anh-huong-en-cac-du-an-1214637.html

Mai Ngoc Chau, Boudreau J (2019) Chinese exporters dodge tariffs with fake made-in-Vietnam labels. https://www.bloomberg.com/news/articles/2019-06-10/vietnam-cracks-down-on-chinese-made-goods-being-shipped-to-u-s

Malesky E (2017) The Viet Nam provincial competitiveness index: Measuring economic governance for private sector development. In Viet Nam Chamber of Commerce and Industry and United States Agency for International Development, 2016 Final Report. Ha Noi: VCCI & USAID

Maruichi D, Abe M (2019) Corruption and the business environment in Vietnam: implications from an empirical study. Asia Pacific Policy Stud 6(2):222–245

McCullough EB (2015) Labor productivity and employment gaps in Sub-Saharan Africa. The World Bank, Washington DC

Ministry of Foreign Affairs Vietnam (2020) 2019 achievements in foreign affairs: Bravery and spirit of the Vietnamese. http://www.mofa.gov.vn/vi/nr040807104143/nr111027144142/ns191231095843

Ministry of Planning and Investment of Vietnam (2020) Brief on foreign direct investment of 2019. http://www.mpi.gov.vn/en/Pages/tinbai.aspx?idTin=45020

Newman C, Narciso G, Tarp F, Vu XN (2009) The role of technology, investment and ownership structure in the productivity performance of the manufacturing sector in Vietnam. Working Paper. Dublin

Ngoc Hoang (2020) EVFTA will create new gateway for market diversification. https://www.rmit.edu.vn/news/all-news/2020/may/evfta-will-create-new-gateway-for-market-diversification

Ngoc Thuy (2019) State firms contribute 28% to Vietnam's GDP in 2018. http://www.hanoitimes.vn/economy/2019/04/81e0d5bf/state-firms-contribute-28-to-vietnam-s-gdp-in-2018/

Nguyen Minh (2018) Stop the "hot and cold" situation. https://dantri.com.vn/dien-dan/cham-dut-tinh-trang-tren-nong-duoi-lanh-2018082907514597.htm

Nguyen Quoc Suu (2018) When will we end the "hot and cold" situation? http://www.tapchicongsan.org.vn/Home/Binh-luan/2018/51828/Tren-nong-duoi-lanh-den-bao-gio.aspx

Nguyen Tuyen (2018) Vietnam has a deficit of more than US$150 billion when doing business with China. https://dantri.com.vn/kinh-doanh/viet-nam-tham-hut-hon-150-ty-usd-khi-lam-an-voi-trung-quoc-20180523073003674.htm

Nguyen TQ, Pham HC, McClelland R (2020) Participating and upgrading in global value chains: The case of small and medium enterprises in Vietnam. In: Macdonald R (ed) The Economy and Business Environment of Vietnam. Springer, Singapore, pp 75–92

OECD (2015) The participation of developing countries in global value chains: Implications for trade and trade policy. https://www.oecd.org/countries/gabon/Participation-Developing-Countries-GVCs-Policy-Note-April-2015.pdf

Ōizumi K (2013) Aging in Asia: When the structure of prosperity changes: Oriental Life Insurance Cultural Development Center

OSMEP (2015) White paper on small and medium enterprises in Thailand 2015. http://164.115.27.49/eng/index.php/data-alert/alert/report-smes-year/report-year

Party General Secretary (2007) Nghị quyết Hội nghị lần thứ ba Ban Chấp hành Trung ương Đảng khoá IX về tiếp tục sắp xếp, đổi mới, phát triển và nâng cao hiệu quả doanh nghiệp nhà nước. http://tulieuvankien.dangcongsan.vn/van-kien-tu-lieu-ve-dang/hoi-nghi-bch-trung-uong/khoa-ix/nghi-quyet-hoi-nghi-lan-thu-ba-ban-chap-hanh-trung-uong-dang-khoa-ix-ve-tiep-tuc-sap-xep-doi-moi-phat-trien-va-640

Phuc Long (2019) Mekong Delta is only 0.8 m above sea level, evacuating risk of 12 million people. https://tuoitre.vn/dbscl-chi-con-tren-muc-nuoc-bien-0-8m-nguy-co-di-tan-12-trieu-nguoi-20190905133103014.htm

Pressello A (2017) The Cambodian conflict and the polarization of Southeast Asia: Japan's response, 1978–1980. Japan and the shaping of post-Vietnam War Southeast Asia. Routledge, Abingdon, pp 97–136

Quynh Trang (2019) Vietnam's labor productivity is still far behind Thailand. https://vnexpress.net/nang-suat-lao-dong-viet-nam-van-thua-xa-thai-lan-3963931.html

Restrepo P (2015) Skill mismatch and structural unemployment. Massachusetts Institute of Technology Job Market Paper, 1–94

Riedel J (2015) Lessons for last comers from Vietnam's transition. Journal of Southeast Asian Economies, 125–139

Riedel J, Turley W (1999) The politics and economics of transition to an open market economy in Viet Nam, OECD Development Centre Working Papers, 152, Paris: OECD Publishing. https://doi.org/10.1787/634117557525

Robles R (2019) Chinese vessel mainly to blame for sinking of Philippine boat in South China Sea, but Filipino crew had 'deficiencies': Leaked report. https://www.scmp.com/week-asia/article/3016428/g20-osaka-china-india-and-russia-draw-close-has-trump-overplayed-his-hand

Shultz CJ, Le K (1993) Vietnam's inconsistencies between political structure and socio-economic practice: implications for the nation's future. Contemporary Southeast Asia, 179–194

Stolnitz GJ (2017) The demographic transition: from high to low birth rates and death rates. Population Growth. Routledge, Abingdon, pp 30–46

Tatarski M (2018) New climate change report highlights grave dangers for Vietnam. https://news.mongabay.com/2018/10/new-climate-change-report-highlights-grave-dangers-for-vietnam/

The Saigon Times (2019) Yuan devaluation expected to put Vietnam's exports at risk. https://english.thesaigontimes.vn/70414/yuan-devaluation-expected-to-put-vietnam%E2%80%99s-exports-at-risk.html

Tran Van Tho (2015) Việt Nam 40 năm qua và những năm tới: Cần một nền kinh tế thị trường định hướng phát triển. Thời đại mới - Tạp chí nghiên cứu & thảo luận (33)

Transparency International (2019) Corruption perception index 2019. https://www.transparency.org/cpi2019

Tri HT, Dao P, Van Ninh N, Sipko J (2017) Analyzing the impact of FDI on Vietnam living environment. ICFE 2017:279

Truong Dinh Tuyen (2019) In Vietnam Thoi Chuyen Doi So. Hanoi: NXB The Gioi

Truong Q, Rowley C (2017) The network-based economy in Vietnam: Business networks in context and over time. Business Networks in East Asian Capitalisms. Elsevier, Amsterdam, pp 307–329

Tung Nguyen (2019) Vietnam c.bank predicted to keep VND stable amid CNY devaluation. http://www.hanoitimes.vn/economy/2019/08/81e0da50/vietnam-c-bank-predicted-to-keep-vnd-stable-amid-cny-devaluation/

Turner M, O'Donnell M, Kwon S-H (2017) The politics of state-owned enterprise reform in South Korea, Laos, and Vietnam. Asian Perspective 41(2):181–184

UNCTAD (2018) World investment report [Press release]. https://unctad.org/en/PublicationsLibrary/wir2018_en.pdf

UNDP. (2015) Country report: 15 years achieving the Viet Nam Millennium Development Goals. https://www.vn.undp.org/content/vietnam/en/home/library/mdg/country-report-mdg-2015.html

UNDP (2019) Productivity and competitiveness of Vietnam's enterprises. Summary report, 1

United Nations (2013) World population prospects 2012—Revision—Highlights and advance tables. United Nations—Economics and Social Affairs, New York, NY

US Department of the Treasury (2019) Macroeconomic and foreign exchange policies of major trading partners of the United States. https://home.treasury.gov/system/files/206/2019-05-28-May-2019-FX-Report.pdf

Vietnam Plus (2018) SOEs failed to disclose business information to be punished. https://en.vietnamplus.vn/soes-failed-to-disclose-business-information-to-be-punished/127807.vnp

VietnamNet (2019) Formosa meets standard three years after pollution incident: environment ministry. https://vietnamnet.vn/en/sci-tech-environmennt/formosa-meets-standard-three-years-after-pollution-incident-environment-ministry-553519.html

VnEconomy (2019) Ứng phó thương chiến Mỹ-Trung: "Tránh thành thị trường xuất khẩu hàng thừa". http://vneconomy.vn/ung-pho-thuong-chien-my-trung-tranh-thanh-thi-truong-xuat-khau-hang-thua-20190908234728916.htm

VnExpress. (2016) In modern Vietnam, a high-tech economy is a future far away. VnExpress International. https://e.vnexpress.net/news/business/in-modern-vietnam-a-high-tech-economy-is-a-future-far-away-3479103.html

Vu HD (2018) Firm's absorptive capacity: the case of Vietnamese manufacturing firms. Review Of Economic Perspectives 18(3):301–325

Ward O (2019) How foreign firms are destroying Vietnam's environment. https://www.aseantoday.com/2017/01/how-foreign-firms-are-destroying-vietnams-environment/

Wendy C, Obert P (2018) Vietnam's future job—Leveraging megatrends for greater prosperity. The World Bank—IBRD DA, Washington DC

Werner A, Simmons C (2009) Impact of sea-level rise on sea water intrusion in coastal aquifers. Ground Water 47:197–204. https://doi.org/10.1111/j.1745-6584.2008.00535.x

World Bank & MPI (2016) Vietnam 2035 report: Toward prosperity, creativity, equity, and democracy. https://www.worldbank.org/en/news/infographic/2016/02/23/vietnam-2035-toward-prosperity-creativity-equity-and-democracy

World Bank (2013) Skilling up Vietnam: preparing the workforce for a modernmarket economy. Vietnam Development Report 2014—World Bank

World Bank (2017) Global Value Chain Development Report 2017: Measuring and Analyzing the Impact of GVCs on Economic Development. https://openknowledge.worldbank.org/handle/10986/11866

World Bank (2017) Vietnam: Enhancing enterprise competitiveness and SME linkages—Lessons from international and national experience. https://openknowledge.worldbank.org/handle/10986/28488

World Bank (2020). Vietnam overview. https://data.worldbank.org/country/vietnam

Xuan Nguyen (2019) Cái chốt 1% ở dự án Cát Linh – Hà Đông. https://vietnamnet.vn/vn/tuanvietnam/tieudiem/cai-chot-1-o-du-an-cat-linh-ha-dong-553145.html

Zhou L (2019) Giant China crane ship turns up near Vietnamese coast. https://www.scmp.com/news/china/diplomacy/article/3025729/giant-china-crane-ship-turns-near-vietnamese-coast

Chapter 3
Public Administration Reform: Efforts and Reality

Effective public administration is considered an important driving force in the social-economic development of nations. Constant changes in the demand and expectations of citizens, competitiveness of business environment and advanced technology force governments around the world to stay focused on their reform agenda. In this chapter, the efforts and reality of Vietnam's public administration reform (PAR) for the past two decades will be discussed. The transition from a command economy to a more market-based economy has necessitated a new model of public administration. The ambitious agenda and the reality of PAR in Vietnam for the last two decades suggest more must be done for Vietnam to realize its potential and achieve its development goals. The chapter is organized as follows. The background information and the evolution of PAR in Vietnam since 2001 will first be presented with specific objectives, achievements and lessons learned for further improvements. The subsequent section presents the general assessment of the PAR limitations, existing problems of public administration in Vietnam. The root causes of problems facing public management in Vietnam will be investigated in the third section. Overall, the analysis in this chapter will help policy makers to identify solutions for improvement-needed areas by providing a background of PAR in Vietnam, its ambitious agenda over the past two decades and the root causes of the existing problems.

3.1 Background of Public Administration Reform in Vietnam

Administrative reforms of Vietnam have been recognized as an important part of the overall national reform progress since 1986 (ADB 2011; London 2014; World Bank and MPI 2016). While considerable efforts from the government have associated market reform with economic growth, PAR plays a key role in transforming Vietnam's economy from centrally planned to market-based (Pham and Vu 2018; World Bank

J. Walsh et al., *The Political Economy of Vietnam's Industrial Transformation*, SpringerBriefs in Political Science,
https://doi.org/10.1007/978-981-16-0151-4_3

and MPI 2016). To be more specific, it has effectively shown its role in economic decentralization and ensuring good standards of governance. In other words, initiatives implemented during the reform related to public, social and economic infrastructure as well as improving the regulatory framework to facilitate better governance were included to enhance the economic growth rate, stimulate the development of the private sector and constrain corruption for increasing the state's accountability.

The government's efforts in PAR have been shown in the last two decades with master programs (MP) clearly defined in two consecutive periods, being the 2001–2010 MP PAR and the 2011–2020 MP PAR. For each period, there have been certain achievements and remaining problems that need to be addressed. The remainder of this section will accommodate a discussion on some general issues regarding objectives, specific programs, outcomes and lessons learned from the two periods of PAR.

In 1999, the government undertook a comprehensive review of PAR, which showed the limited results achieved since 1986 (Painter 2003). It was pointed out that the legacy of the central planning system remains embedded in the state public administration. That system was thus unable to meet the demands of the new (market-based) management mechanism under new conditions (Prime Minister of Vietnam 2001b). An MP was therefore designed for 2001–2010 (Prime Minister of Vietnam 2001a). This was viewed as an ambitious and comprehensive plan in which four major reform areas were set out including institutions, organizational structure, civil service and public finance reform.

The plan specified nine objectives to be achieved during the period of 2001–2010, with strong focus on administrative process simplification, accountability, coordination, transparency, professionalism, corruption reduction and compartmentalization reduction in the preparation of legal documents (Vasavakul et al. 2009). This wide-ranging plan was divided into two periods: 2001–2005 and 2006–2010. There were seven action programs corresponding to those objectives, and each program was sub-divided. Different central government agencies were charged with supervising these programs (Eduardo et al. 2011).

Concerning actual specific achievements, the 2001–2010 reform did make some progress towards public administration improvement. Important laws were issued in this period, such as the Law on Government Organizing, on People's Councils and People's Committees, and on Cadres and Public Servants. Although these achievements have not met the demand of the process of development, they were nonetheless good in view of the level of economic development (Ketels et al. 2010). In addition, thousands of procedures have been cancelled or improved to bring better services to citizens (Thuy Chung 2011). These are noticeable positive changes as a result of the PAR process. Moreover, the significant reform in government structures is also worth noting. As can be seen in Table 3.1, a reduction in the number of ministries, ministry-level and government agencies decreased gradually from 1986 to 2011 and achieved 18 ministries, ministry-level and 4 government agencies in the 12th government (National Assembly 2010).

Table 3.1 Number of ministries, ministry-level agencies and government agencies. *Source* Author's compilation

From	Ministries, ministry-level agencies	Government agencies
1986	67	48
1992	27	31
1997	23	25
2002	26	14
8/2007	22	8
8/2011	18	4

To simplify administrative procedures from the central to commune level, the Ministry of Home Affairs (MOHA) standardized one-stop shop mechanisms, generally known as "một cửa một dấu" in Vietnamese. Given that all types of one-stop shop separated citizens from the officials who handled their requests, they were expected to help curtail abuses of power. It was also believed that the "one-door" principle would help restructure the internal work processes of state agencies.

Taking a further step to investigate the reform progress deeply, the 2001–2010 PAR outcome generally did not meet the targets set in the master program; the outcomes could be viewed as the initial accomplishment. In certain areas, administrative procedures remain cumbersome, inconsistent and irrational, causing difficulties for people and enterprises (National Assembly Standing Committee 2010). One of the major objectives of the MP PAR 2001–2010 was to build a force of capable cadres and public servants who would play an important role in the process of nation-building and development. However, after ten years of implementation, the National Assembly Standing Committee concluded (National Assembly Standing Committee 2010) that the capacities of those in public service remain limited and that inappropriate and corrupt behaviour towards citizens are not isolated occurrences. This problem is possibly caused by three main reasons, which include low salary in the public sector, patronage and nepotism, and overstaffing, to be discussed in later parts of this chapter.

From the first ten-year experience in PAR with recognizable achievements and existing limitations, the government has extracted five lessons to be learned for further improvements in the next period (Vietnam Government 2011). It is stated that PAR is a broad task, involving many fields, which must be carried out synchronously in the overall renovation of the political system, in association with the construction and reorganization of the Party and the reform of the state apparatus. Next, there must be a close combination between PAR and the economic reform in every prospect and every locality, which is expected to create a mutually promoting effect between PAR and the renovating economy management framework. Moreover, PAR is also considered a sensitive and difficult task, which requires steering agencies with consistent views, principles and practical action plans in each sub-period. This leads to another lesson suggesting that administrative reform must be implemented synchronously from top to bottom with respect and encouragement for boosting initiatives at local and grass-root levels. Finally, administrative reform must stem from Vietnamese practices with

Vietnamese characteristics, traditions and identities. At the same time, learning from the knowledge and experience of other countries about the organizing approaches and management activities for proper application needs to be considered.

Inheriting the experience and practical lessons from the 2001–2010 PAR, Vietnam Government has announced the Master plan for a new phase of PAR (2011–2020) in the Resolution 30c/NQ-CP (Vietnam Government 2011). The focus of administrative reform in the following 10 years is associated with institutional reform, formulating and improving the quality of cadres, civil servants and public employees, reforming the wage policy in order to create a real motivation for cadres, civil servants and public employees to perform their duties with quality and efficiency, improving the quality of administrative and public services (Vietnam Government 2011). In addition to the four reform areas of 2001–2010 PAR, the MP for the 2011–2020 period lists two more areas that make it different. These areas are associated with renovations in administrative procedures and national administration system modernization (The Steering Committee for Administrative Reform 2016).

Regarding recognized achievements in the 2011–2015 period, administrative procedure renovation is one of the key areas that attract concerns and direct guidance from the central government. The Prime Minister has signed various documents to enhance the effectiveness of monitoring public administrative processes. The implementation of PAR has simplified administrative procedures. Every year, the review and simplification of administrative procedures have helped to liberate social resources and enhance national development (The Steering Committee for Administrative Reform 2016). Furthermore, in the government's emerging efforts to modernize the public administration system, information technology infrastructure is built to a quality standard that basically meets the operational requirements of state agencies. Most of the ministries, branches and localities have implemented the official email system. The increasing use of electronic documents as ordered by the Prime Minister under Directive No. 15/CT-TTg (Prime Minister of Vietnam 2013) has generated expected results. About 80% of administrative documents are exchanged electronically at both central and local levels. The number of ministry-level administrative agencies, provincial-level professional agencies and district-level administrative units using local area networks (LANs) to exchange work in 2011 reached nearly 2,900 units. By 2015, that number has reached nearly 3,500 units, with an increase of 20.7% (The Steering Committee for Administrative Reform 2016).

Vietnam's government has recently introduced a new agenda for PAR. Nguyen Xuan Phuc, the Prime Minister, in his inaugural address on 7 April 2016, committed to transforming the "command government into an enabling government (*chính phủ kiến tạo*)". The Prime Minister has ordered "discipline, righteousness, action, creativity, breakthrough, and efficiency" as new objectives of administrative reform, which aims to place Vietnam on the list of most favourable business environments in ASEAN. The instruction has been given to provinces/cities and sectors by Prime Minister Phuc at the meeting held by the Government's Steering Committee for Administrative Reform in 2019 (Thu Hoa 2019). This reveals the government's commitment to improving initiatives gradually to enhance the effectiveness of the PAR agenda.

To sum up, the PAR of Vietnam has endured for nearly two decades with gradually improved MPs for two consecutive periods (2001–2010 and 2011–2020). Improvements have been well recognized and lessons have been learned. However, problems still exist, which will be identified in the next section.

3.2 Problems of Public Management in Vietnam

Despite efforts indicated by ambitious plans and objectives, which were recognized by some initial achievements of PAR for nearly two periods with gradually renovating initiatives, there are still problems associated with public management. Defining problems with public management in Vietnam is, therefore, an essential step towards further PAR to boost national growth.

Issues associated with public management in Vietnam are said to be inhibitors of the general business environment development (Maruichi and Abe 2019). Previous studies have suggested several angles to look at when investigating a business environment's attractiveness. The World Economic Forum (WEF) in 2016, via their study of 16 indicators of business environment analysis, suggests major issues possibly inhibiting the development of the appeal of Vietnam's business environment (WEF 2016). These are mostly associated with public management, including inefficient government bureaucracy, government instability and poor work ethic in the public labour force. In another research effort, the 'Vietnam 2035: Towards Prosperity, Creativity, Equity, and Democracy' report reviewed existing problems with Vietnam's public management in four major dimensions, which were state effectiveness, commercialization of the state, unmeritocratic administration and lack of accountability of the state to citizens (World Bank and MPI 2016). There is a common theme of perspectives when looking at the performance of Vietnam's public management, which relatively aligns the study of WEF with the one conducted by the World Bank. Consequently, in this section, the problems of Vietnam's public management will be addressed in more detail, regarding the four dimensions mentioned above.

3.2.1 The Low Effectiveness of the State

The term 'effectiveness' refers to the state's capacity to sustain good practices of public governance and administration to facilitate rapid socio-economic development. Regarding this demand, an effective state needs to take effort in removing obstacles associated with complicated public administrative processes and fighting against corruption at all levels (World Bank and MPI 2016). If a state is said to be ineffective or quite ineffective, there should be several weaknesses in operational terms that need to be considered. Operational weaknesses of the state in Vietnam can be understood in terms of contradictory or unclear regulations causing confusion for businesses, conflicting mandates of state agencies, corruption and selective law enforcement (*ibid.*).

The state's ineffectiveness is presented by difficulties that businesses must face regarding public administrative processes. Despite recognizable improvements in the business registration process, the informal payments and the cumbersome administrative procedures in land management or site clearance emerge as notable problems for many companies (PCI Report 2019). In detail, 53.6% of companies participating in the survey of PCI noted that they had to make informal payments, while 48.0% of FDI enterprises admitted that they spent an average of 24 million VND on unofficial fees to get construction permits in 2019 (*ibid.*). Vu Tien Loc—President of the Vietnam Chamber of Commerce and Industry, representing the business community of Vietnam, states that the government and ministries should make more effort in centralizing solutions to remove bottlenecks and barriers for new business entries regarding public administrative processes (Bao Ngoc 2020).

As a further step to broadening the understanding of the low ineffectiveness of the state in the case of Vietnam, the below reasons are provided. Firstly, government institutions in Vietnam are fragmented vertically, which makes it sometimes possible for local authorities to go against directives from the central government. This partially explains why the performance of public administration in many provinces is still low despite considerable efforts from the central government to guide and mandate (Pincus 2015). Secondly, Vietnam's public policies are not fully guided and inspired by the market rationality. That is, it is said that regulations still favour state-owned or state-connected companies. Unevenly enforced property right between private and public firms can be taken as an example (Thomsen 2011). Thirdly, the government's decision-making process shielded from public scrutiny represents another condition that holds back the development of effective state operational activities (World Bank and MPI 2016).

3.2.2 Corruption and Informal Payments

Corruption, as generally used, is the term applied for describing illegitimate use of power by cadres or public servants for their own advantage. This definition covers several activities including 'bribery, extortion and conspiracies to defraud public funds' (Palmier 2003, p. 73). In this section, the current scenario of corruption in Vietnam will be presented, together with "petty corruption" *(tham nhũng vặt)* as a phenomenon resulting from Vietnamese culture.

In the global fight against corruption, it is generally agreed that fraudulent corruption should be treated as a crime like others (Kidd and Richter 2003). However, the work of detecting corruption is challenging for various reasons. First, corrupt activities are conducted in a secret mode, which helps avoid leaving sufficient evidence and trails for investigators (Balaniuk et al. 2013). To be more specific, there is not always an obvious victim in corruption cases as the transaction only occurs between two or more involved people with the intention of abusing power for personal advantage. This leads to the second challenge for detecting corruption, which is that conspirators in fraud do not have the intention to denounce one another as both parties seem to be satisfied (Lee and Oh 2007). For enterprises, such corruption creates opportunities for them to gain a high return on money expended when generated shortcuts will help save time, efforts and capital with merely slight risk. As a result, these attractions should not be overlooked.

Corruption is considered a serious economic problem, which tends to coexist with a high growth rate in the early stages of developing countries. Vietnam has been consistently ranked low in the global Corruption Perceptions Index (CPI) from 2015 to 2019, standing 96th in its global perception of corruption index in 2019, which implies that the country has not made significant progress (Transparency International 2019). For the period from 1996 to 2014, 51% to 70% of Vietnamese firms have reported that they must pay bribes to access better and faster government services. They tend to consider those informal or irregular payments a normal and widely accepted practice when doing business in the country (PCI Report 2014). Moreover, as shown by data from the Global Competitiveness Index in 2014, Vietnam has the worst score in irregular payments and bribes in East Asia and Pacific, followed by Indonesia, the Russian Federation and Thailand (WEF 2014).

That corruption in economies with a high growth rate seems to be endemic suggests an interesting perspective. This perspective argues that economic growth is facilitated by corruption in that it provides a path to bypass a bureaucracy characterised by slow movement and progress (Anh et al. 2016). This establishes a mindset for Vietnamese firms that corruption is a part of doing business. However, it surely comes with a cost. The long-term negative impacts that corruption has on market efficiency, investment and political stability must be considered (World Bank and MPI 2016). The gradually embedded perception of inequality and unfairness resulting from public power abuse can cause social tension undermining state legitimacy.

Petty corruption implies the phenomenon that Vietnamese businesses have to pay a small facilitation cost to lubricate public administrative processes such as license applications or business registrations. The phenomenon can be understood as an informal payment. In recent years, there has been an optimistic view on the reduction of informal payments. According to the recent PCI report, despite the fact that there are still 53.6% of Vietnamese firms having to settle informal payments, the number in 2019 is the lowest for the last five years (PCI Report 2019). Party General Secretary and State President Nguyen Phu Trong said in a meeting that "To get work done, people must pay informal fees. Petty corruption like scabies is very itchy and annoying" (Quang Phong 2015). The Vice Prime Minister of Vietnam, Truong Hoa Binh, states that people and businesses have not been able to eliminate the psychology of giving gifts, even bribes to get work done. This partially resulted from citizens' past experience with difficulties, troubles and harassment generated by cadres or civil servants, which forced them to accept that making progress with their work will require sacrifice (Thu Hang 2019). Mr. Binh emphasized the government's effort to remove this phenomenon as its impacts are also considerable, no less than big corruption, which may undermine and erode the confidence and reliability of people in the state.

3.2.3 Unmeritocratic Administration

According to Barakat et al. (2012), an unmeritocratic public administration system refers to a scenario in which the government fails to hire capable public servants with a high standard of ethical behaviour who are strongly motivated to carry out the government's functions. It is indicated by international experience that building a meritocratic system of public administration requires a long time and substantial efforts from different levels of the government (Dahlström et al. 2012). Features and consequences of an unmeritocratic administration system will be elaborated in this section.

In Vietnam, the development of a meritocratic system has been largely hindered by two specific features, which are the traditionally well-embedded recruitment protocol and fragmented public human resource management. For the first feature, it is noticeable that despite the government's efforts during PAR to mandate open recruitment for all technical positions since 2008, patronage relationships and seniority rather than merit are still setting the basis for recruitment and promotion (Vu et al. 2019). The second feature represents the fact that public human resource management responsibility is assigned to three different entities including the Central Committee Secretariat, Organization Commission of the Party and the government (Shen and Cox 2017). The fragmented responsibility leads to several issues related to picking the right people. These two features are considered root causes for the unmeritocratic administration of Vietnam.

The unmeritocratic system is said to be constituted by corruption. Side payments and personal relationships involved in public job distribution can result in considerable damage to bureaucratic capacity. The study of the World Bank and Government Inspectorate of Vietnam in 2016 on factors that influence promotion in the public sector show that 60% of the respondents reported bribes being paid to get government jobs. Moreover, from the perspective of citizens and firms, personal connections are viewed as the main contributing factors to success in the public sector, which is followed by material incentives (*ibid.*). This situation tends to be more serious. Another recent study shows that about 62% of respondents agreed that they pay bribes to work in the public sector (PAPI 2019). Widespread concern over nepotism in the public sector at all levels has been recently discussed in Vietnamese presses and some of those cases will be investigated in the reasons and root causes section of this chapter.

3.2.4 *The Lack of Accountability in the Public Sector*

The state-citizen relationship is essential to an effective state. Relationship capacity must be represented by the freedom of people to participate in the decision-making processes and accountability of the government regarding truthfulness and transparency in reporting results of its performance (Pradhan 2019). In order to achieve proper accountability standards, it is highly recommended to open formal channels to the government for citizens' participation in decision-making processes. In fact, Vietnam has an excellent level of formal civic participation with tens of thousands of social organizations and a third of the Vietnamese population are members of one of those groups (Markussen 2015). Through the channel of these organizations, citizens can support government social programs, provide social services when the government fails to do so and monitor actions of the authorities.

Despite the significant number of civic organizations, citizens' participation is still constrained. The Government of Vietnam does not seem to consult in a substantive way with those organizations. As a result, civil society organizations in Vietnam have not been seen as an active tool to influence public policies (World Bank and MPI 2016). This also leads to limited standards of transparency, which hinders citizens' ability to hold the government accountable. Additionally, the governance practices of Vietnam, like those of other countries with a state-dominated history, do not feel comfortable with state activities being open to discussion and criticism. Consequently, the development of a democratic society is profoundly affected and market efficiencies are undermined. The Global Competitiveness Index (World Economic Forum 2019) indicates that in the first pillar, institutions, Vietnam ranked 89th with a score of 49.8, which was lower than that of Singapore, Malaysia, Indonesia, Brunei, Thailand and the Philippines.

The National Assembly of Vietnam has gradually regained its role of strengthening the position of citizens. However, there is still room for further improvements with the aim of legislative exercising and oversight of the government (Malesky and Schuler 2009). In fact, the National Assembly is still not empowered enough to establish proper policy to monitor the government's activities (World Bank and MPI 2016). Moreover, it is the irrational and problematic structure of representation that creates a bias towards accepting whatever is proposed by executives. Consequently, Vietnam falls into the group of countries with poor effectiveness in legislature in monitoring and limiting the power of government, ranking 85th in the world (World Justice Report 2020). As a result, the expected transparent relationship between citizens and the state is not ensured as the National Assembly, the supreme formal organization representing citizens' interests, cannot guarantee its capability to oversee the government.

Several existing problems of public administration in Vietnam have been reviewed in this section. Most of them have been embedded in the nature of public management in Vietnam, which undermine the development of socio-economy. In order to come up with proper initiatives as solutions to these problems, it is important to investigate the causes which will be presented in the following section.

3.3 Root Causes of Existing Problems of Public Management in Vietnam

In this section, root causes of existing problems in public administration of Vietnam will be discussed as challenges that the country needs to overcome for further achievements according to the agenda of PAR—MP. The discussion begins with an overview of the relationship between key institutions of Vietnam's political system, which has been said to generate opacity in the accountability of the Party and State. Subsequently, four other contributing factors of patronage and nepotism, overstaffing in the public sector, low salary and poor quality of public servants are presented.

3.3.1 Opaque Accountability of the Party and State

The mismatch between responsibility and power in the position of the Prime Minister, especially in respect of key government appointments, has been criticized by senior Party and State leaders. For example, Party intervention in the Prime Minister's right under law to establish a facade undermines the performance of the Prime Minister and the government.

While the National Assembly increasingly calls upon the government to be responsible and accountable, the right of the Prime Minister to nominate government members is greatly restrained by law and Party intervention. Legislation provides that the Prime Minister is elected or dismissed by the National Assembly at the State President's request. According to Article 4 of the law of Government organization, the Prime Minister is the Head of the Central Government and is accountable to the National Assembly. In theory, the Prime Minister has the right to appoint and dismiss Deputy Prime Ministers and ministers, subject to the National Assembly's approval (Vietnam National Assembly 2001). In reality, the Prime Minister alone does not have the right to select government members because the Central Party makes the selection before the list is sent to the National Assembly to be voted upon (Khiet and Le 2007; Xuan Trung 2005). In addition, the choice of candidates for government members is narrow and limited to members of the Party Central Committee.

Similarly, Ministers have insufficient powers to appoint their assistants. This gives rise to the rejection of individual responsibility. Although Ministers are responsible for their portfolios and are accountable to the Prime Minister, they do not have the direct right to choose their deputies. Further, there are cases where leaders are 'afraid' of their deputies (Khiet Hung and Le 2007) because the latter are nominated and supported by more powerful individuals or a Party body like the Party Commission for Organization and Personnel or Party Secretariat (Tien Phong News 2008). As Mai Ai Truc (Xuan 2005), a former Minister for Natural Resources and Environment, concluded when he was under pressure at Question Time in the National Assembly, 'responsibilities are unlimited, but power is limited.' A former Prime Minister, Phan

Van Khai, contended that it is impossible to hold ministers responsible for problems in their ministry because they do not have the right to appoint their deputies (Xuan Trung 2005).

Considerable impacts from Party intervention have made policy decision-making and implementation in the government not autonomous. The general motto is that the 'Party leads, State manages.' However, mechanisms to make that arrangement work seem lacking (Gillespie 2006). Despite the growing separation of Party and State in the 1990s (Painter 2003), Party and State figures during the 2000s have called for further separation. Early resistance to the Party's intervention in State management became well known through a memo by Prime Minister Vo Van Kiet to his Politburo colleagues, whereby he demanded a clear division in the functions of Party and government. Vo Van Kiet's arguments, published in a domestic newspaper, have been translated as (Riedel and Turley 1999:37):

> Party and State functions need to be separated more clearly. The party must cease passing its directives through party committee secretaries and instead pass them through the government chain of command, allowing government officials to take full responsibility for implementation. A 'law-governed State' must supplant organizational structures that had originated in war, and State agencies for their part must cease their involvement in commercial activities. Failure to take these steps in the past is the reason many correct positions and policies of the Party and laws of the State cannot be implemented.

The opaque accountability of the Party and State leads to a lack of effectiveness in operation when responsibility and power are not clearly distinguished between the two. Additionally, the overstaffing issue in the public sector, discussed below, leads to difficulties in public human resource management regarding challenges to the fair distribution of liveable income to cadres and civil servants. This generates a big gap in public employees' contributions and their actual remuneration. Reality has shown that corruption and informal payment come as consequences of this gap.

3.3.2 Patronage and Nepotism

The issue of family connections swaying politics in Vietnam is under the central government's investigation. The statement of Vietnam Prime Minister, Nguyen Xuan Phuc, regarding his commitment to push the investigation into allegations of nepotism has been in the national headlines since 2017. He has instructed the Ministry of Home Affairs and local authorities to dismiss appointments of any bureaucrat influenced by nepotism (Vietnam News 2016). This goes along with national efforts to stop the eroding effect on public confidence of offering key positions based on family connections.

The problem of nepotism and patronage in public recruitment has been well-embedded in the culture of public management in Vietnam. The Governance and Public Administration Performance Index (PAPI) of Vietnam in 2017 confirmed that informal payments and personal relations have played important roles for people who wish to pursue careers in the public sector. Since 2012, nepotism and corruption in the public sector have drawn the attention of policymakers as systemic problems. In a recent report, PAPI once again emphasized that nepotism together with bribery in recruiting public employees serves as two contributors to corruption in state employment and deterioration of efficiency in public administrative services (PAPI 2018). According to Eduardo et al. (2011), a patronage-based system of public administration specifies the focus on private and personal interests rather than transparency for the common good. In other words, nepotism leads public administration on the basis of personal ties including loyalty to a relative or patron rather than the system itself. In this kind of system, public officials tend to help themselves and their family members when they are still in power. This scenario has been quite commonly seen in countries such as China in the time of Mao Tse Tung and the Soviet Union during the time of Stalin (Eduardo et al. 2011). In Vietnam, despite many efforts since the enactment of reforms mandating open recruitment for technical positions in 2008, the recruiting and promoting processes are still conducted with the priority on patronage relationships and seniority rather than merit (World Bank and MPI 2016). It is said that distributing jobs based on relationships and unofficial payments rather than merit is the strongest destructive force for bureaucratic capacity, which makes room for corruption in practices of public human resource management. There is a common saying for people pursuing public sector careers, which is that personal connections are perceived as the top advantage for people who want to pursue a career in public sector and the main contributory factor for success, followed by material incentives—"*Nhất quan hệ, nhì tiền tệ*" (World Bank and The Government Inspectorate of Vietnam 2016).

Moreover, the issues of patronage and nepotism in public recruitment and promotion definitely create unmeritocratic administration. As a general understanding, in an unmeritocratic system, recruitment and promotion are driven by relationships and loyalty rather than qualifications, efforts and potential contribution. As a result, the quality of public servants will not be ensured and the public sector's accountability will be distorted. These problems and root causes suggest existing weaknesses associated with capabilities to reform. Consequently, there is a need for gradually reviewing the PAR MP in order to adjust and adapt to the emerging requirements of a developing economy.

3.3.3 Overstaffing in the Public Sector

Overstaffing in the public sector is another concern. Earlier, Painter (2005) shows that Vietnam has the highest percentage of public servants, compared to Indonesia, Thailand, the Philippines, and South Korea, comprising 5.5% of the total workforce. This number increased to 10% in 2015, which made Vietnam's public sector among the largest in Southeast Asia (Cunningham and Pimhidzai 2018; Viet Tuan 2018). The increasing percentage of public servants attracts attention and critics from policymakers regarding its impacts on the public performance and productivity of the whole economy. To be more specific, they notice that if the productivity level of the public sector decreased, the impact would be detrimental as talent was drawn from the private sector, which is potentially more productive (Cunningham and Pimhidzai 2018).

As reported by local media, the problem of excess state employees does exist. In total, Vietnam's government has approximately 2.8 million people on the payroll (Viet Tuan 2018). According to findings of government auditors, 57,175 public workers on the government payroll are not needed and they urged state departments to consider tightening their control over human resources (Thanh Lan 2018). Additionally, the number of managers in the public sector appears to crowd out those people who actually do the groundwork. Take the recent investigation of Vietnam's government auditors in Vinh Phuc province as an illustration, where it was reported that 38 of 45 members of the province's department of education and training are managers and 9 of 12 people working for the province's home affairs department hold management positions (Tuoitre News 2017). A possible implication of this scenario is that the larger proportion of highly paid positions may lead to unequal income distribution in the public workplace and the efficiency of salary budget utilization has deteriorated.

Acknowledging the problem of excess public employees, the central government of Vietnam is considering plans and initiatives to enhance the effectiveness and efficiency of public workforce management. By 2019, many agencies at all levels have responded to the order in 2017 from Vietnam's Prime Minister, Nguyen Xuan Phuc to reduce public staff numbers annually by 1.5%–2% (Hoang Dien 2017; VNA 2019). Overall, Vietnam's public agencies were planning to cut down over 4,000 officers, public employees and civil servants in 2019, which makes the total public staff reduction reach 44,510 since 2015. This number is constituted of 5,500 governmental workers and 39 civil servants (VNA 2019). This has resulted from the efforts of ministries, sectors and localities to focus on reviewing, adjusting and consolidating all functions and tasks entitled to their subordinate units to reduce overlaps.

Despite recognizable efforts, Vietnam still has a long way to go regarding the agenda reducing the size of the public workforce. Continuing these workforce efficiency-enhancing initiatives will make room for deploying better management and salary reform policies.

3.3.4 Low Salaries in Public Sector Jobs

A well accepted reason for the slow progress in public workforce quality improvement is low salaries. In Vietnam, state workers were paid VND 1.3 million (US$57) a month as basic wage rising to VND 1.39 million in July 2018 and VND 1.49 million in July 2019 (National Assembly 2018; Thanh Lan 2018; Vietnamnet 2019). The basic wage sets a base for minimum monthly payment calculation by multiplying it with a coefficient determined by seniority and qualifications. Since 2016, Vietnam has considered reforming policies for public servant remuneration, which increased the minimum wage in the public sector by 5% in 2016 and 7.4% in 2017 (Hoang Manh 2015; Vietnam Government 2017). However, the public workforce has consistently complained of low earnings.

It is reported that the salaries of many public officials are not sufficient to cover the basic cost of living. Thang Van Phuc, the former Deputy Minister of Home Affairs, pointed out that Vietnam's government salaries cover only 50% to 60% of basic living cost (Truong 2020; Tuoitre News 2016). Under the payroll protocol in 2019, Vietnam's President and Party Secretary earned only approximately VND19.3 million (US$833) a month. This was equal to the amount earned by a small company's head accountant at that time. In fact, despite the modest earnings, a sizable number of Vietnamese cadres and public servants can still manage expensive houses and cars. This scenario implies that low official payment forces public workers to look for other income sources, which possibly leads to embezzlement and corruption. It is difficult for public servants to fight against the temptation of material goods when they possess certain powerful positions to offer benefits for others in-need but their monthly incomes are very low (Nguyen and van Dijk 2012). There have been many cases of corruption recorded during the development of Vietnam. Vu (2010) identified six prominent types of public work where informal and illegal income is often generated, including positions with the (1) right to allocate land to enterprises, (2) the right to approve projects of different types, (3) the right to ask banks to lend money to enterprises, (4) the right to issue fines, (5) the right to recommend appointments or rewards and (6) the authority to decide the level of tax that individuals or enterprises should pay.

Initiatives associated with financial autonomy in public agencies have shown some slight improvements in incomes public workers. In compliance with Decree 43/2006/NĐ-CP, the implementation of the financial autonomy mechanism has marked a strong transformational impact on public non-business agencies' self-responsibility in organizing and arranging apparatus, payroll and financial resources to complete assigned tasks. This also helps promote all capabilities of those agencies in providing high quality public services to society, increasing revenue sources to solve income problems for officials and employees (Vo and Lofgren 2016). Practical results revealed that workers at public agencies with financial autonomy have witnessed gradual increases in their monthly incomes, which were said to be generated by efforts in optimizing revenue sources, enhancing internal control and service quality while saving costs (Painter 2005). However, there are still limitations associated with the financial autonomy progress, which concern the inequality in the incomes of employees in wholly autonomous units, partially autonomous units and units fully funded by government budget. This suggests an unfair reflection of employee contributions (The Steering Committee for Administrative Reform 2016). In 2016, the government issued Decree 16/2015/NĐ-CP, which replaced Decree 43/2006/NĐ-CP of 2006. However, the low salaries of state workers remain problematic. This limits the quality of public service and invites corruption.

3.3.5 Poor Quality of Public Servants

One of the overall objectives formally written into the 2001–2010 PAR MP was to "…build a force of cadres and public servants who have appropriate capacities and ethical qualities able to meet the requirements of nation building and development" (Prime Minister of Vietnam 2001b). After ten years of working towards this goal, this target has not yet been achieved. There remain a number of steep hurdles on the path to a strong force of public service. It is not just in isolated cases that cadres and public servants have delayed their work, misbehaved with citizens and indulged in corruption. In general, the capacities of public servants, particularly in local governments, remain limited (National Assembly Standing Committee 2010; Nguyen Khac Giang 2019).

Labour inefficiency and poorly qualified staff in many public agencies are still problematic. This idea was emphasized by Deputy Prime Minister Truong Hoa Binh at a meeting organized by the Ministry of Home Affairs on January 15th, 2019. Mr. Binh pointed out that there are shortcomings in the work of Vietnam's administrative system, which resulted from the poor quality of cadres and public servants, regarding delays in issuing legal documents, partial monitoring and a lack of staff performance evaluations (Vietnamplus 2019).

The government's progress in promoting the civil service is slowly being implemented, as reported by local media. This is largely caused by the fact that the quality of cadres and public servants fails to meet requirements for development despite recognizable improvements as discussed above. The shortcomings in public civil service quality was said to be mainly caused during the transformational process from centrally-planned economy to market economy. This implies that Vietnamese cadres and civil servants need to possess essential skills in absorbing new values and standards, which would help establish suitable administration models for the country's current situation (Le Vinh Tan 2018). In fact, it is noted that in order to achieve proper levels of development, renovation and international integration, Vietnam still needs to take further steps regarding training and capacity building to ensure the required adequacy of public human resources. A view on public workforce quality enhancement commonly shared by policy makers suggests linking quality improvement initiatives with effective salary reform policy for public workers. Better salary packages are said to represent a tool for government to attract competent candidates, which then fosters the overall transformation through the approach of establishing a talent-based civil service.

Looking on the bright side, the quality of Vietnamese cadres and civil servants has been gradually improved regarding their qualifications, competence, professional knowledge and management skills. This trend is accompanied by the properly ensured public employment structure of ranks, age and gender. According to Cunningham and Pimhidzai (2018), in 2014, 80% of Vietnamese public sector employees had a post-secondary education and 52% were university graduates. This represents the government's efforts in renewing public servant recruitment to ensure openness, fairness and transparency in upholding competitiveness in selecting leaders and managers. However, taking a deep look into the current scenario of public service quality, there is still plenty of room for further improvements in public workforce capacity (Le Vinh Tan 2018).

3.4 Conclusion

In the effort to offer an overview of PAR in Vietnam, this chapter has gone through the phases of administration reform with specified objectives, action plans and achievements. Despite consistent commitment, problems associated with public administration quality still exist. This chapter has identified key problematic areas in public administration in Vietnam. It is widely accepted by researchers and practitioners that these problems will distort the socio-economic development of the country. Furthermore, root causes to existing problems have also been examined including opaque accountability of the state and party, patronage and nepotism in recruitment as well as promotion in the public sector, overstaffing, low salary and the poor quality of public servants.

Vietnam still has a long way to go in removing problems with the public administration system, which will make the whole socio-economic mechanism run smoothly. This requires stronger efforts in learning from the last two periods of PAR, consolidating experience and enhancing workforce capabilities to adapt to new challenges of developing a digital government, digital economy and digital society.

Acknowledgements The authors would like to thank Tran Pham Khanh Toan and Thanh Vu for their research assistance.

References

ADB (2011) Southeast Asia Sector Assessment and Roadmap. Viet Nam: Public Sector Management. Retrieved from Hanoi. https://www.adb.org/sites/default/files/linked-documents/cps-vie-2012-2015-ssa-08.pdf

Anh NN, Minh NN, Tran-Nam B (2016) Corruption and economic growth, with a focus on Vietnam. Crime Law Social Change 65(4–5):307–324

Balaniuk R, Bessiere P, Mazer E, Cobbe P (2013) Collusion and corruption risk analysis using Naïve Bayes classifiers advanced techniques for knowledge engineering and innovative applications (pp. 89–100). Springer

Bao Ngoc (2020) PCI-2019 announcement: More than 50% of businesses have to pay unofficial fees. Retrieved from https://tuoitre.vn/cong-bo-pci-2019-hon-50-doanh-nghiep-phai-tra-chi-phi-khong-chinh-thuc-20200505101739268.htm

Barakat S, Evans M, Zyck SA (2012) Karzai's curse–legitimacy as stability in Afghanistan and other post-conflict environments. Policy Studies 33(5):439–454

Cunningham W, Pimhidzai O (2018) Vietnam's Future Jobs—Leveraging Mega-trends For Greater Prosperity—Main Report. Retrieved from http://documents.worldbank.org/curated/en/973841543238555966/pdf/129380-v4-WB-Vietnam-Future-Jobs-Main-report-English.pdf

Dahlström C, Lapuente V, Teorell J (2012) Public administration around the world. Good government: the relevance of political science, 40–67

Eduardo KAJ, Vu K, Nguyen A (2011) Improving efficiency and effectiveness of public administration, management and governance: what can viet nam learn from international experience? Retrieved from http://www.depocen.org/ckfinder/userfiles/files/publications/Books/Improving%20efficiency%20and%20effectiveness%20of%20public%20administration_Vietnam%20(English).pdf

Gillespie JS (2006) Transplanting commercial law reform: developing a 'Rule of Law' in Vietnam: Ashgate

Hoang Dien (2017) Thủ tướng Chính phủ chỉ thị đẩy mạnh tinh giản biên chế. Retrieved from http://vpcp.chinhphu.vn/Home/Thu-tuong-Chinh-phu-chi-thi-day-manh-tinh-gian-bien-che/20171/20757.vgp

Hoang Manh (2015) Tăng lương công chức, viên chức: Có thể sau 1/7/2016? Retrieved from https://dantri.com.vn/viec-lam/tang-luong-cong-chuc-vien-chuc-co-the-sau-1-7-2016-20151103010427091.htm

Ketels CH, Nguyen DC, Nguyen TTA, Do HH (2010) Vietnam competitiveness report 2010. Retrieved from https://www.economica.vn/Portals/0/Documents/Vietnam%20Competitiveness%20Report%202010Eng.pdf

Khiet H, Le AD (2007) Former president of the National Assembly: PM must be entitled to choose his cabinet members. Retrieved from http://www.tuoitre.com.vn/tianyon/Index.aspx?ArticleID=204066&ChannelID=3

Kidd J, Richter F-J (2003) Fighting corruption in Asia: Causes, effects and remedies: World Scientific

Le Vinh Tan (2018) Ongoing reform of the civil service in Vietnam. Retrieved from http://vietnamlawmagazine.vn/ongoing-reform-of-the-civil-service-in-vietnam-6108.html

Lee S-H, Oh KK (2007) Corruption in Asia: pervasiveness and arbitrariness. Asia Pacific J Manag 24(1):97–114

London JD (2014) Politics in contemporary Vietnam Politics in Contemporary Vietnam (pp. 1–20). Springer

Malesky E, Schuler P (2009) Paint-by-numbers democracy: the stakes, structure, and results of the 2007 Vietnamese national assembly election. J Vietnamese Studies 4(1):1–48

Markussen T (2015) "Social and political capital in rural Vietnam," WIDER Working Paper Series wp-2015-087, World Institute for Development Economic Research (UNU-WIDER)

Maruichi D, Abe M (2019) Corruption and the business environment in Vietnam: Implications from an empirical study. Asia Pacific Policy Studies 6(2):222–245

National Assembly Standing Committee (2010) Report on implementation of Master Plan of Public Administration Refrom in 2001–2010 Retrieved from http://www.na.gov.vn/htx/Vietnamese/default.asp?sAction=DETAIL_CONT&intDocID=1362#QMX5AARrgE11

National Assembly (2010) Report 378/BC-UBTVQH12 on implementation of Master Plan of Public Administration Refrom in 2001–2010 Retrieved from http://quochoi.vn/hoatdongcuaquochoi/cackyhopquochoi/quochoikhoaXII/kyhopthutam/Pages/van-kien-tai-lieu.aspx?ItemID=1715

National Assembly (2018) Resolution 70/2018/QH14: Ve du toan ngan sach nha nuoc nam 2019

Nguyen Khac Giang (2019) Nhi lai viec danh gia can bo. Retrieved from https://www.thesaigontimes.vn/295476/nhin-lai-viec-danh-gia-can-bo-.html

Nguyen TT, Van Dijk MA (2012) Corruption, growth, and governance: Private vs. state-owned firms in Vietnam. J Banking Finance 36(11):2935–2948

Painter M (2003) Public administration reform in Vietnam: problems and prospects. Public Administr Develop 23(3):259–271

Painter M (2005) Public Administration Reform in Vietnam: foreign transplants or local hybrids? Asian Socialism and Legal Change, 267

Painter M (2006) Sequencing civil service pay reforms in Vietnam: transition or leapfrog? Governance 19(2):325–346

Palmier L (2003) Corruption in context. Fighting Corruption in Asia: Causes, Effects and Remedies, 73–90

PAPI (2018) The Viet Nam Provincial Governance and Public Administration Performance Index 2018 Measuring Citizens' Experiences, 2018. Retrieved from http://papi.org.vn/eng/wp-content/uploads/2019/03/2018PAPIREPORT_EN_FINAL.pdf

PCI Report (2014). ietnam Provincial Competitive Index 2014. Retrieved from https://pcivietnam.vn/uploads//VN-Bai-trinh-bay/PCI-2014_Bai-trinh-bay_VN_DauAnhTuan.pdf

PCI Report (2019) Vietnam Provincial Competitive Index 2010. Retrieved from https://pcivietnam.vn/an-pham/bao-cao-pci-2019-ct172

Pham B, Vu H (2018) Poverty Reduction in Vietnam and the role of public administration. J Contemporary Asia 49:1–13. https://doi.org/10.1080/00472336.2018.1515368

Pincus J (2015) Why doesn't Vietnam grow faster? State fragmentation and the limits of vent for surplus growth. J Southeast Asian Econ, 26–51

Pradhan U (2019) Multi-Ethnic Citizens in a Multi-Ethnic State: Constructing State-Citizen Relations Through 'Difference' in the Adivasi Janajati Scholarship Programmes in Nepal. South Asia: J South Asian Studies 42(5):937–953

Prime Minister of Vietnam (2001a) PM Decision 112/2001/QĐ-TTG on computerization of state administrative management for the period 2001–2005. Hanoi: Vietnam Government. Hanoi: Vietnam Government

Prime Minister of Vietnam (2001b) PM Decision 136/2001/QD-TTg on approval of the Master Plan on Public Administration Reform for the period 2001–2010. Vietnam Government—Hanoi

Prime Minister of Vietnam (2013) Directive No. 15/CT-TTg: Enhancement of administrative procedure control urged. Vietnam Law and Legal Forum Retrieved from http://vietnamlawmagazine.vn/directive-no-15-ct-ttg-enhancement-of-administrative-procedure-control-urged-2454.html

Quang Phong (2015) Party General Secretary: Petty corruption is similar to scabies, itchy and annoying. Retrieved from https://dantri.com.vn/xa-hoi/tong-bi-thu-tham-nhung-vat-nhu-ghe-ruoi-rat-kho-chiu-1437968185.htm

Riedel J, Turley W (1999) The Politics and Economics of Transition to an Open Market Economy in Viet Nam. OECD Development Centre Working Papers, No. 152, OECD Publishing, Paris. https://doi.org/10.1787/634117557525

Shen J, Cox A (2017) Human Resource Management in China and Vietnam Routledge Handbook of Human Resource Management in Asia (pp. 295–313). Routledge

Thanh Lan (2018) 57,000 civil servants in Vietnam hold redundant positions: audit. Retrieved from https://e.vnexpress.net/news/news/57-000-civil-servants-in-vietnam-hold-redundant-positions-audit-3698955.html

The Steering Committee for Administrative Reform (2016) Tài liệu hội nghị: Sơ kết công tác cải cách hành chính giai đoạn 2011-2015 và triển khai kế hoạch cải cách hành chính giai đoạn 2016-2020. Retrieved from https://www.moha.gov.vn/DATA/DOCUMENT/2016/08/Tai%20lieu%20SK%20CCHC/Bao%20cao%20SK%20CCHC%20(in%202%20mat)%20resize.pdf

Thomsen L (2011) Business-state relations in the differentiated private sector in Vietnam: access to capital and land. Asian J Socl Sci 39(5):627–651

Thu Hang (2019) Phó Thủ tướng: Tham nhũng vặt không kém gì tham nhũng lớn. Retrieved from https://vietnamnet.vn/vn/thoi-su/chong-tham-nhung/pho-thu-tuong-tham-nhung-vat-khong-kem-gi-tham-nhung-lon-545409.html

Thu Hoa (2019) Vietnam accelerates administrative reform. Retrieved from https://vovworld.vn/en-US/current-affairs/vietnam-accelerates-administrative-reform-725821.vov

Thuy Chung (2011) Government reviews the 10 years of public administration reform. Retrieved from http://vietnamnet.vn/vn/chinh-tri/15024/chinh-phu-nhin-lai-10-nam-cai-cach-hanh-chinh.html

Tien Phong News (2008) Truong Chi Trung and Dinh Tien Dung no longer hold the position of Vice Minister. Retrieved from http://www.tienphong.vn/Thoi-Su/135316/Hai-ong-Truong-Chi-Trung-va-Dinh-Tien-Dung-thoi-giu-chuc-Thu-truong.html

Transparency International (2019) Corruption Perceptions Index 2018. Retrieved from https://www.transparency.org/cpi2019

Truong TH (2020) The effects of corruption on the human capital accumulation process: Evidence from Vietnam. Econ Transition Inst Change 28(1):69–88

Tuoitre News (2016) Salary of Vietnam's public servants only meets 50% of living standards. Tuoi Tre Newspaper. Retrieved from https://tuoitrenews.vn/society/37523/salary-of-vietnams-public-servants-only-meets-50-of-living-standards

Tuoitre News (2017) 38/45 công chức Sở Giáo dục tỉnh Vĩnh Phúc là lãnh đạo. Retrieved from https://tuoitre.vn/38-45-cong-chuc-so-giao-duc-tinh-vinh-phuc-la-lanh-dao-1374775.htm

Vasavakul T, Thai L, Van Le (2009) Public Administration and Economic Development in Viet Nam: Remaking the Public Administration for the 21st Century. Retrieved from https://www.undp.org/content/dam/vietnam/docs/Publications/25527_05_PARECONDEV_FINAL.pdf

Viet Tuan (2018) Vietnam to cut civil servants by 5,510 next year. Retrieved from https://e.vnexpress.net/news/news/vietnam-to-cut-civil-servants-by-5-510-next-year-3793110.html

Vietnam Government (2006) Decree No. 43/2006/ND-CP. Vietnam Law & Legal Forum Retrieved from http://vietnamlawmagazine.vn/decree-no-43-2006-nd-cp-1868.html

Vietnam Government (2011) Decree 30c/NQ-CP: Ban hành Chương trình tổng thể cải cách hành chính nhà nước giai đoạn 2011–2020. Retrieved from http://vanban.chinhphu.vn/portal/page/portal/chinhphu/hethongvanban?class_id=2&_page=1&mode=detail&document_id=152523

Vietnam Government (2017) Decree 47/2017/NĐ-CP. Thu Vien Phap Luat Retrieved from https://thuvienphapluat.vn/van-ban/lao-dong-tien-luong/Nghi-dinh-47-2017-ND-CP-muc-luong-co-so-doi-voi-can-bo-cong-vien-chuc-luc-luong-vu-trang-301465.aspx

Vietnam National Assembly (2001) Law on Organization of Government

Vietnam News (2016) Nepotism must be abolished in Việt Nam. Retrieved from https://vietnamnews.vn/opinion/300513/nepotism-must-be-abolished-in-viet-nam.html#8gvUTo5XDCSbST9w.97

Vietnamnet (2019) Basic salary for civil servants increases as of July 1. Retrieved from https://vietnamnet.vn/en/society/basic-salary-for-civil-servants-increases-as-of-july-1-546682.html

VNA (2019) Over 4,000 officials, public employees to be made redundant in 2019. Retrieved from https://en.vietnamplus.vn/over-4000-officials-public-employees-to-be-made-redundant-in-2019/153806.vnp

Vo M, Lofgren K (2016) Autonomy of Public service delivery agencies in Vietnam and OECD: a comparative institutional perspective. Asian J Public Affairs 9(1):21–42

Vu A, Plimmer G, Berman E, Sabharwal M (2019) Managing employee performance in transition economies: a study of Vietnamese public organizations. Public Administ Develop 39(2):89–103

Vu (2010) Salary and 'informal income' of public servants. Retrieved from http://doanhnhansaigon.vn/article-print.aspx?articleId=1047411

WEF (2014) The Global Competitiveness Report. Retrieved from http://www3.weforum.org/docs/WEF_GlobalCompetitivenessReport_2014-15.pdf

WEF (2016) The Global Competitiveness Report 2016–2017. Retrieved from Geneva: http://www3.weforum.org/docs/GCR2016-2017/05FullReport/TheGlobalCompetitivenessReport2016-2017_FINAL.pdf

World Bank and MPI (2016) Vietnam 2035 Report: Toward Prosperity, Creativity, Equity, and Democracy. Retrieved from https://www.worldbank.org/en/news/infographic/2016/02/23/vietnam-2035-toward-prosperity-creativity-equity-and-democracy

World Bank, and The Government Inspectorate of Vietnam (2016) Managing Conflict of Interest in the Public Sector: Law and Practice in Vietnam. Retrieved from http://documents.worldbank.org/curated/en/580601478253123042/pdf/AUS11340-WP-p153692-PUBLIC-ConflictofinterestEN.pdf

World Justice Report (2020) Rule of Law Index 2020. Retrieved from https://worldjusticeproject.org/our-work/research-and-data/wjp-rule-law-index-2020

Xuan Trung (2005) Leaders should have the right to hire and fire. Retrieved from http://www.tuoitre.com.vn/Tianyon/Index.aspx?ArticleID=110158&ChannelID=3

Chapter 4
From State to Market: Evolving Ownership and Corporate Governance in Vietnam

One of the central issues in analysing political economic change requires understanding the ownership model of the productive sector in economy. Consequently, this chapter provides insights about the development of ownership types (public vs. private) and corporate governance rules in Vietnam. In addition, it provides an analysis of the current challenges for regulators and firms in strengthening governance mechanisms in order to deepen capital markets, encourage private ownership and facilitate foreign investment.

4.1 Introduction

Chief of the reforms undertaken in Vietnam since the Renovation (*Đổi Mới*) Policy initiated in 1986 was the creation of a "Socialist-oriented market economy." In practice, this meant the gradual injection of market mechanisms into what was previously a centrally-controlled command economy. To achieve the transition, the reform entailed a shift from 100% government ownership to a partially privately-owned economy, starting in 1992 with a "demutualization" of the state-owned enterprises (SOEs) and transformation into shareholding or limited liability companies. Alongside this new form of private ownership, the government promulgated the Vietnam Enterprise Law and Securities Law in 2005, which provided the basic rules for the establishment, management and operations of these new privately-owned companies. The Enterprise Law also provided the basic principles of corporate governance mechanisms regulating the relationship between the owners and managers of privately-owned firms. These rules were a necessity for the privately-owned firms since, in SOEs, the owner is the manager. Now, there is a large number of SOEs being transformed into shareholding companies or limited liability companies through the equitization programme.

J. Walsh et al., *The Political Economy of Vietnam's Industrial Transformation*, SpringerBriefs in Political Science,
https://doi.org/10.1007/978-981-16-0151-4_4

The relative newness of the corporate governance rules in Vietnam explains partly why these corporate governance rules are still regarded as of lower quality standards than that of peers in the region, despite several revisions of the Enterprise and Securities Laws. The weakness of the current corporate governance system in Vietnam has detrimental effects on securities markets' depth and behaviour, investment opportunities for individual and savings organizations, the ability to structure an efficient pension system, the attractiveness of foreign direct investment (FDI) and lastly, firm performance. What will the future hold? There are encouraging signs that regulators are recognizing the need to strengthen corporate governance rules in Vietnam. The State Securities Commission has in 2019 overhauled the Code of Corporate Governance ("hard laws") in order to align the rules for Vietnamese securities markets in line with international practice. In addition, these rules are becoming increasingly supplemented by "soft laws" (codes of conduct) emanating from new institutions in Vietnam, such as the Vietnam Institute of Directors (VIOD). With the combination of stronger regulation and a more widespread adoption of codes of corporate governance conduct, Vietnam can catch up with international best practice in the medium term.

4.2 The Structure of the Economy in Vietnam Before 1945

Prior to French colonization in the mid-19th century, Vietnam had been a self-sufficient, village-oriented economy (autarky) in a feudalist society. Its economy relied almost entirely on agriculture, with a minority of the population working as artisans (e.g. goldsmiths, silversmiths and iron casting), traders and miners. Different dynasties throughout the history of Vietnam were occupied with conflicts with neighbouring kingdoms, including China from the North and Champa and Khmer empires from the South. The economy was interrupted with feudalist warfare with only short periods of development during temporary times of peace. During these stable periods, Vietnamese dynasties tried to maintain a centralised power by setting an autocratic social order and economic structure. An agricultural autarky with limited domestic and international trade made agricultural land the most valuable asset, which was de facto owned by the ruler. To uphold his absolute power, the emperor periodically redistributed large landholdings and eventually, the Nguyen dynasty abolished all private landholding and ended all nascent trading with the West (Jamieson et al. 2019).

By the late 19th century, Vietnam, together with Laos and Cambodia, was turned into a French colony known as Indochina.[1] The French administration built public infrastructure (such as railroads, canals and highways) and established industries to serve the systematic exploitation of natural resources and labour in the region.

[1]The rising French capitalism demanded new territories for resource by means of colonisation. Meanwhile, the strongly anti-Western emperor of Vietnam (Minh Mang) attempted to end all trading with the West as well as eliminate Western Catholic influences by dismissing all French advisers and executing Catholic missionaries in Vietnam. In 1857, the French used these actions by the Nguyen emperor as an excuse to invade Vietnam and gradually annexed Vietnam, Laos and Cambodia into the so-called French Indochina.

Ownership of agricultural land, industrial plantations, coal mines and factories, as well as any immediate profits from these enterprises belonged to the foreign rulers. Except for a small class of local landlords, no Vietnamese people owned any property or oversaw business entities. The economic structure in colonial Vietnam was set up to benefit the foreign capitalists, while excluding the Vietnamese from enterprise ownership and civil participation.

4.2.1 The Economy Between 1946 and 1975

The oppression by the colonial regime led to a series of national resistance movements throughout the 20th century. Not until 1945, by the end of World War II, was Vietnam able to gain independence and formed a free state under the name Democratic Republic of Vietnam (*Việt Nam Dân Chủ Cộng Hòa).* From 1946 to 1954, the French reinstated its protectorate in South Vietnam by reviving industries and maritime trade. However, after being defeated at the Battle of Dien Bien Phu, the French government agreed to a cease-fire at the Geneva Conference of 1956. The Geneva Accords divided Vietnam into the communist North (Democratic Republic of Vietnam) and the non-communist South (Republic of Vietnam), to be united by a national election which was postponed indefinitely under US pressure.

The Ministry of Industry and Trade (MOIT) established a mixed ownership system which included public and private industrialisation efforts in North Vietnam up until the mid-1950s. The new North Vietnamese government nationalized many former French factories, infrastructure and heavy industries, such as coal and tin mines and rail roads. At the same time, privately owned small and medium sized enterprises were allowed to operate and produce goods to address the domestic supply shortage and provide employment. Domestic trading of commodities resembled a free market mechanism, albeit under state supervision and partly for military supply.

In 1958, the North Vietnamese economy was reformed into the centrally planned model, mandating state and collective ownership of all productive assets. At the same time, the economy in the South followed free market principles, while being strongly supported by foreign aid with the US as the principal donor. The opposite ideologies underpinning the North and South exacerbated the ongoing conflict of the Vietnam War, leading eventually to reunification on 30th April, 1975 with the withdrawal of the US from the South and the victory of the North Vietnamese communist government.

4.3 Ownership of Enterprises from 1975 to 1986

At the end of the war, the Communist Party of Vietnam (CPV) extended the centrally planned economic model, which was based on a Soviet economic model, to all provinces in Vietnam. State ownership replaced all private businesses that used to operate in the South (Phan et al. 2018). Only SOEs in the manufacturing and trading sectors and collective cooperatives in the agricultural sector were considered legal entities in the economy, while private ownership was seen as "the enemy of socialism" (Zhu et al. 2008:160).

Deficiencies in production causing, among others, food shortages soon after, prompted the Government to experiment with limited economic liberalizations from the late-1970s (Rama 2014). For example, some local agricultural cooperatives contracted plots of land to peasants and paid them according to their crop yields (also known as the illicit contractual system), which proved successful in promoting production and thus was adopted nation-wide with the official Directive-100 in 1981 (Ngo 1993). These liberalization initiatives led to a decision to place the economy firmly on a transitional path from the socialist planning model to the market system (Doan and Nguyen 2013). The 6th National Congress of the CPV announced the top-down "*Đổi Mới*" reform program which shifted the centrally planned economy to a socialist-oriented market economy.

4.4 Post *Đổi Mới* Ownership

Six years after announcing the *Đổi Mới* reform, the government launched the privatization initiative under the name 'Equitization Programme', in line with the intended transition towards a market-based economy. The equitization (full or partial privatisation) of SOEs in 1992 was triggered by two factors. First, the sustained operational and financial inefficiencies of SOEs were noted by policy makers. Second, the continuing presence of SOEs appeared to hinder the growth of private enterprises by accumulating capital and favoured treatment from the government (Nguyen and Freeman 2009). Transferring ownership of state enterprises to private owners was framed as a policy to support market efficiency and fair competition.

In reality, the government has taken careful steps in the equitization process, starting with a *trial phase* (1990–1992) and an *accelerated phase* (1998–2006) which saw a surge of divested SOEs in preparation for Vietnam's accession to the WTO. Privatisation of almost 60% of all equitized SOEs happened during the peak four years between 2003 and 2006, although these were mostly small and medium enterprises (Le 2017; Tran and Holloway 2014).

4.4.1 Fewer but Larger SOEs

The figure below shows the sharp decrease in the number of enterprises with over 50% of state capital from 2003 to 2006, which reached a plateau in 2007. Only after 2007 did the government officially consider privatizing some of the remaining large SOEs. The complexity of these organisations partly slowed down the process. In the same period from 2007 to 2015, the government also emphasized restructuring and re-categorisation of state-owned business entities according the proportion of

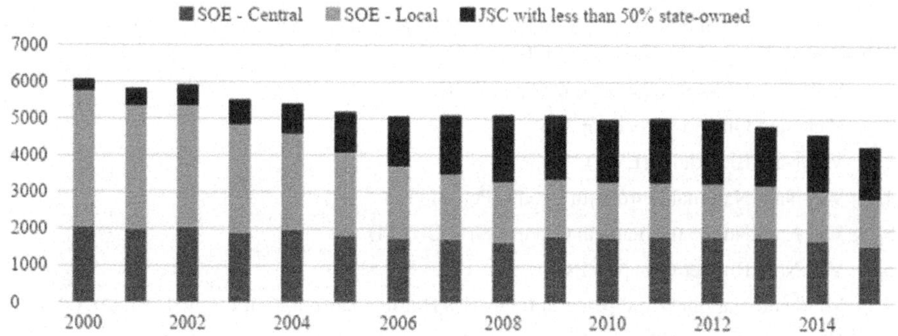

Fig. 4.1 Number of SOEs from 2000–2015. *Source* GSO Statistical Yearbook (multiple years)

charter capital owned by the state (100%, from 50% to under 100%, and less than 50%) (Fig. 4.1).[2]

While the number of SOEs has declined steadily since the launch of the Equitization Programme (from 6,334 to 4,251), most of the equitized enterprises have been small and owned by provincial authorities, while the number of centrally-owned state enterprises hardly decreased (from around 2,000 to 1,550) since the beginning of the millennium.

Several scholars have considered Vietnam's privatization as an alternative way for the state to retain its authority through continued oversight and interference especially in strategic industries during the marketisation process (Beeson and Pham 2012; Gainsborough 2009; Painter 2008). Besides, part of the Equitization Programme included the consolidation of SOEs into strategic State Economic Groups (SEGs) owned by various ministries. In 2019, management of all SEGs was transferred to the Committee for State Capital Management (CMSC, also known as the "Super Committee"). Table 4.1 provides an overview of these 19 SEGs. According to financial statements as of 2017, the total value of equity of these 19 SEGs exceeded US$43 billion and the total value of assets reached more than US$100 billion. The government plans to retain only three SEGs (PetroVietnam, Electricity of Vietnam and Viettel Military Telecommunications Group) by 2020 (Ha Thu 2018).

The State Capital Investment Corporation (SCIC), technically owned by the Ministry of Finance, is a holding company which serves as a strategic investor in state-owned companies that were handed over by a wide array of government authorities. In the period from 2006 to 2015, 990 SOEs were transferred to SCIC, which is approximately 80% of all those wholly divested. The SCIC intends to retain only 20 enterprises for long-term investment, with the remainder to be privatized in the short to medium term. While those 20 enterprises represent only 10% of the total,

[2]Previously, the Vietnam General Statistics Office (GSO) recorded two types of SOEs by local and central ownership. These include (1) Enterprises with 100% of state capital (2) Limited companies under management of central or local government; (3) Joint stock companies with domestic capital, of which the government shares more than 50% charter capital.

Table 4.1 State Economic Groups under the Management of the Committee for State Capital Management. *Source* Viet Nam News (2018)

1.	State Capital Investment Corporation (SCIC)
2.	Việt Nam Oil and Gas Group (PVN)
3.	Việt Nam Electricity (EVN)
4.	Việt Nam National Petroleum Group (Petrolimex)
5.	Việt Nam National Chemical Group (VINACHEM)
6.	Việt Nam Rubber Group (VRG)
7.	Việt Nam National Coal-Mineral Industries Holding Corporation Limited (VINACOMIN)
8.	Việt Nam Post and Telecommunications Group (VNPT)
9.	Việt Nam Mobile Telecom Services One Member Limited Liability (MobiFone)
10.	Việt Nam National Tobacco Corporation (VINATAB)
11.	Vietnam Airlines
12.	Việt Nam National Shipping Lines (VINALINES)
13.	Việt Nam Railways (VNR)
14.	Việt Nam Expressway Corporation (VEC)
15.	Airports Corporation of Việt Nam (ACV)
16.	Việt Nam National Coffee Corporation (VINACAFE)
17.	Việt Nam Southern Food Corporation (VINAFOOD 2)
18.	Việt Nam Northern Food Corporation (VINAFOOD 1)
19.	Việt Nam Forest Corporation (VINAFOR)

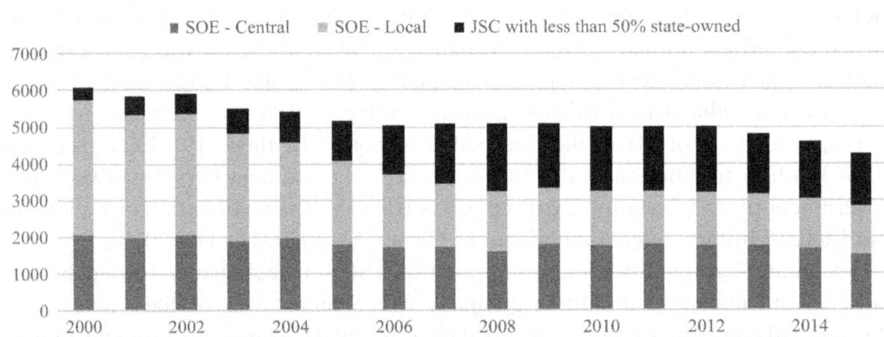

Fig. 4.2 Number of SOEs from 2000–2015. *Source* GSO Statistical Yearbook (multiple years)

they make up more than half of the total asset value of SCIC's portfolio. This divestment strategy reflects the precept of privatizing smaller SOEs while retaining larger enterprises.

The establishment of SEGs and the Super Committee signals an ambition to strengthen the state presence in certain arenas by consolidating the capital and expertise necessary to compete with foreign players (ADB 2015). The movement towards the creation of larger state conglomerates also reflects the political ideal of state-led marketisation, promoting state-owned 'leading enterprises' while simultaneously embracing market reform (Beeson and Pham 2012).

Vinatex is an illustration of such policy. The textile conglomerate had upon its formation in 1995 the mission to implement the state's masterplan in the textile and garment industries. That masterplan consisted of satisfying domestic demand, creating employment and increasing competitiveness in the sector by integration with the global economy. To implement that masterplan, the government had full ownership and managed the company like a government entity (e.g., the Prime Minister had to approve major capital expenditure). Vinatex then became a federation of 53 amalgamated companies, four different accounting units and five research institutions and vocational schools (Fujita 2017). The government provided a host of privileges to Vinatex as an SEG. The state provided "infant industry" measures to protect the SEGs from foreign competition through drastic increases in tariffs, preferential access to finance, guaranteed market outlets through, e.g., requiring other SOEs to purchase the products of an SEG. With a stronger commitment to global and regional economic integration through trade agreements and accession to WTO, these privileges could not be sustained and had to be revoked. The government responded to the increased market pressures by partially privatizing Vinatex's subsidiaries (in 2005) and the holding company (in 2015). In 2019, Vinatex was no longer recognized as an SEG, reflecting its large percentage of private ownership of around 47%.

In reality, state ownership appears to be a burden on the productivity and ability of these firms to innovate and develop capabilities to compete in the marketplace. Most SOEs have goals additional to profit maximization such as employment, social welfare or regional development. These goals are vaguely defined, causing difficulties in embedding them in operating strategies. Additionally, since ownership is in the hands of the state, SOEs do not face the disciplinary function of capital markets, since no one can take over a poorly performing SOE. The state has non-financial incentives to support underperforming SOEs and shield them from bankruptcy. Complex management and reporting structures, especially in large SOEs and SEGs with many unrelated business activities, leads to lower commercial viability.

The inefficiency of SOEs in Vietnam was brought into the public spotlight after the bankruptcy of several large SOEs, notably Vinashin and Vinalines in 2011. Losses resulting from mismanagement of state capital and corruption in SOEs have intensified public pressure for reform and privatisation of SOEs. The increasing budget deficit has also made it more urgent for the government to push forward the privatisation process (Le 2017). Since 2016, a new wave of equitization has taken place, aiming to accelerate the rate of equitization and divestment after relative slowdown between 2011 and 2015.

Meanwhile, the private sector was playing an increasingly important role in the economy. The figure below shows the decline of state-owned and concurrent rise of privately-owned enterprises in the economy in terms of turnover. During 2000 to 2017, the share in turnover of SOEs dropped by around half. At the end of that period, the private sector represented 82% of total turnover. The increased importance of the private sector requires the government to create frameworks for fair competition and good governance, which is discussed below (Figs. 4.3 and 4.4).

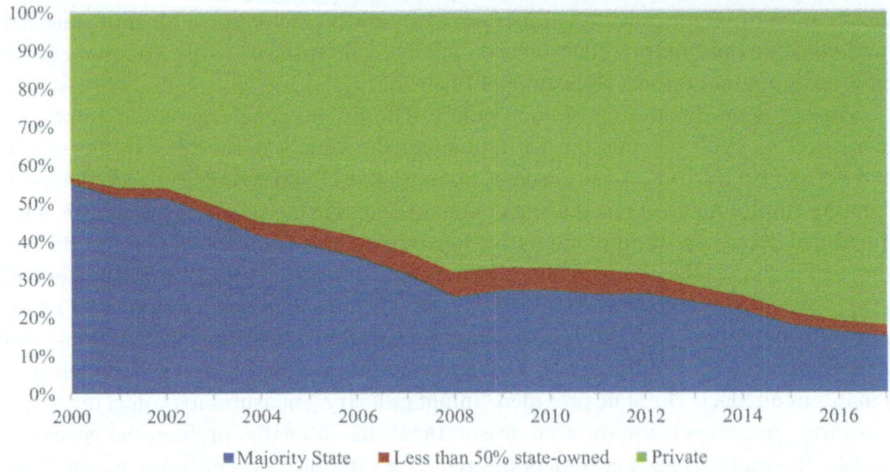

Fig. 4.3 Aggregate Net Turnover from Business by Type of Enterprise. *Source* GSO Statistical Yearbook (multiple years)

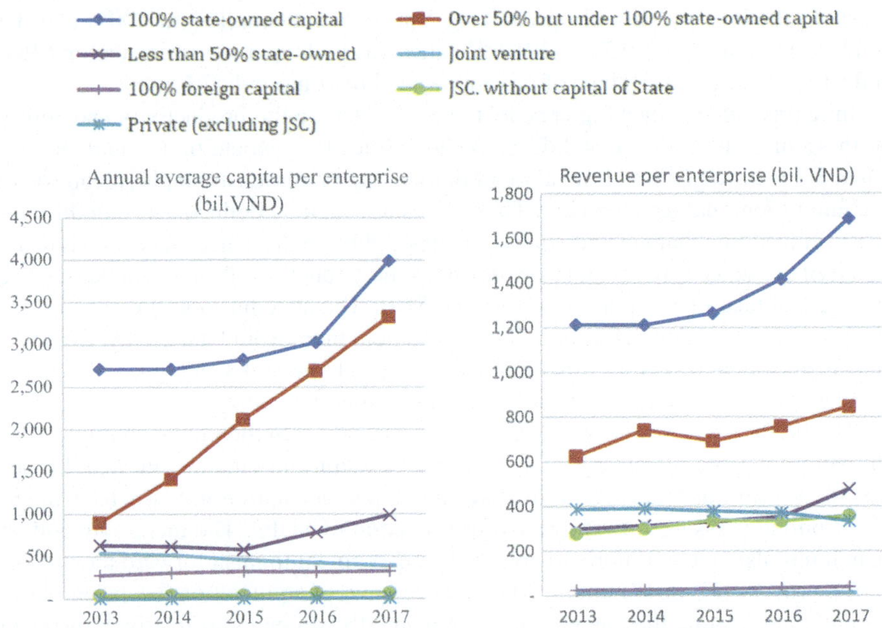

Fig. 4.4 Annual Average Capital per Enterprise (Unit: billion VND). *Source* GSO Statistical Yearbook (multiple years)

4.4.2 A Comparison of State and Non-State-Owned Enterprises

How have SOEs performed in recent years? In terms of size, enterprises with higher state ownership tend to have much higher annual average capital and revenue compared with those without, i.e. privately and foreign owned companies. The average size of these SOEs shows no sign of decrease, despite the falling number of SOEs. This reflects the government strategy to retain the largest enterprises under state ownership.

Figure 4.5 provides an overview of productivity measures of enterprises by ownership type. Some of these measures may seem surprising as they are contrary to prior research about productivity differences across enterprises. Empirical evidence documents that, by and large, SOEs register lower productivity, lower employment and lower post-privatization financial returns (see, e.g., Megginson and Netter 2001). Contrary to that evidence, an average Vietnamese SOE generates higher turnover and profits than a privately-owned firm. In other words, the average SOE is much larger and more efficient than any other non-state-owned enterprise. Interestingly, for SOEs, the size (in turnover) is directly related to the ownership percentage of the state. A wholly SOE, on average, generates twice the revenue per year of a majority state-owned and more than three times that of a minority state-owned enterprise.

Similar patterns can be seen for the profit measure: the average SOE registers higher profits than its privately-owned counterpart. However, it is likely that many of these very large SOEs are exposed to much lower competitive forces than privately-owned firms, thereby causing these superior profits. Examples of this are the state-owned electricity provider Vietnam Electricity (EVN) and the mobile telecoms oligopoly composed of Viettel, Mobifone and Vinaphone. All of these SOEs are highly profitable. The government retains ownership of these large and profitable firms perhaps from an industrial policy motivation (i.e. industries that are deemed strategic to the development or national security of the country). Historically, governments tend to own enterprises in these highly capital-intensive industries such as telecoms, airlines or railways as private enterprises did not get access to the large financial resources required, since only the sovereign borrower did. In terms of profits per employee, which is a common efficiency measure, the picture looks a bit different. A Joint Venture (JV) company registered the highest amount (236 million VND), whereas a 100% SOE declared only 177 million VND per employee despite its larger size and generally less competitive industry structure (Fig. 4.6).

Similarly, JVs display the highest profit margins (11%) as well as return on assets (ROA) of 9% among all enterprise types. Regardless of the percentage of state ownership, SOEs register low profit margins (between 6% and 9%) and ROA (from 2% to 4%). The higher the percentage of state-owned capital, the lower the profit margins, which is contrary to pattern of profit per enterprise shown above. This implies that the SOEs use their assets less efficiently than other private enterprises considering their large size and market power. In addition, their low profit margins indicate a higher

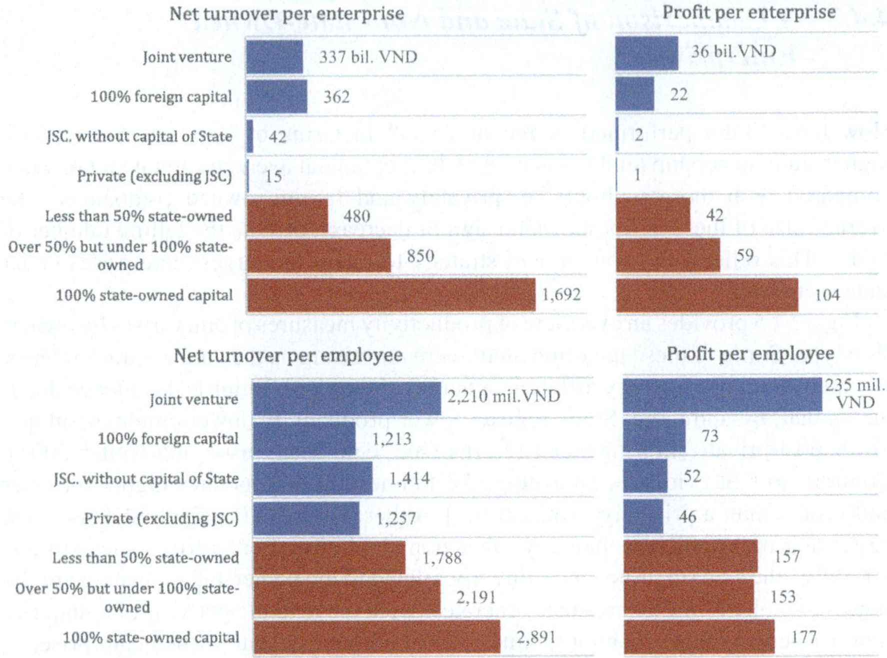

Fig. 4.5 Comparing Productivity Measures in 2017 of Different Types of Enterprise. *Source* GSO (2018)

cost structure compared to privately owned companies. This low asset efficiency of SOEs has been observed in many countries and industries, confirming that state ownership is not only associated with profit maximization principles but, also, with objectives such as employment, political power, regional development or industrial policies. Alternatively, low asset efficiency can also be explained through the market failure lens: fundamentally, SOEs are justified in segments of the economy where market forces are absent (Mühlenkamp 2015). Examples of such market failures include natural monopolies such as Vietnam Railways or the provision of public goods such as by Vietnam Electricity (EVN).

The highest profit margins and efficiency are registered by joint ventures in Vietnam, exceeding those of privately, foreign, or state-owned enterprises according. These metrics illustrate that the combination of capabilities of a foreign partner (such as brand, technology or skills) with capabilities of a domestic JV partner (in particular, market access) creates superior performance.

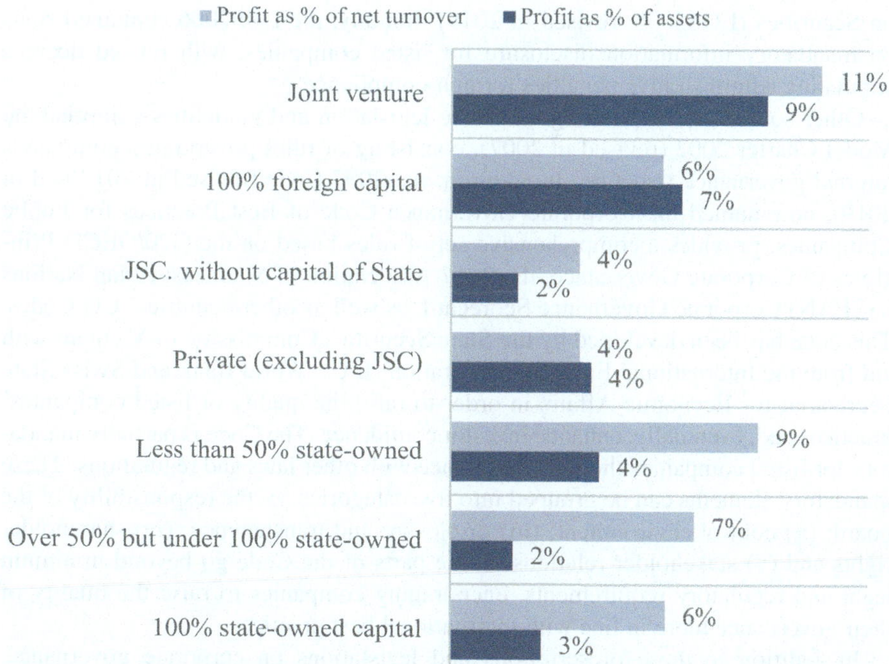

Fig. 4.6 Revenue and Profit per Employee in 2017, by Type of Enterprise. *Source* GSO (2018)

4.5 Evolving Corporate Governance

As the corporate ownership structure and economic policies have evolved since the mid-1980s to give market institutions increasing prominence, so did the legislation and regulation of the governance mechanisms of public[3] and listed companies. Corporate governance frameworks were slowly and somewhat late adopted and implemented in Vietnam. While SOE privatization started in the late 1990s and the first stock exchange was created in 2000 (see Appendix), it was only the Law on Enterprises in 2005 (LOE2005, revised in 2014) that laid the foundations of the Vietnamese corporate governance system. Perhaps this lateness was rooted in the French civil law system on which much of the Vietnamese legislation resides. A civil law system has been shown to engender heavy regulation, less secure property rights and less efficient governments (La Porta et al. 1999)

The LOE2005, relevant to all listed companies in Vietnam regardless of their ownership structure or economic sector, was supplemented in 2006 by the Law

[3]In Vietnam, a public company designates a shareholding company which exhibits one of the following three characteristics: (a) it has made a public offer of shares; (b) it has shares listed on the Stock Exchange or a Securities Trading Centre or (c) has shares owned by at least 100 investors excluding professional securities investors and has a paid-up charter capital of a minimum of ten billion VND.

on Securities (LOS2006, revised in 2019). Initially, the LOS2006 contained rules on mandatory information disclosure for listed companies, with related decrees stipulating administrative penalties for non-compliance.

Other sources of corporate governance legislation and guidelines comprise the Model Charter 2002 (revised in 2007), consisting of rules governing a company's internal governance structure. In addition, the 2007 Code (revised in 2012 and in 2019), now named the Corporate Governance Code of Best Practices for Public Companies, provides a comprehensive set of rules based on the G20/OECD Principles of Corporate Governance, the 2017 Association of Southeast Asian Nations (ASEAN) Corporate Governance Scorecard, as well as other countries' CG Codes. This code has been developed by the State Securities Commission of Vietnam with aid from the International Finance Corporation (IFC), World Bank and Swiss State Secretariat for Economic Affairs in order to raise the quality of listed companies' practices and, eventually, enhance investor confidence. The Code is partially mandatory for listed companies though compliance with other laws and regulations. These mandatory elements can be grouped into five categories: (i) the responsibility of the board; (ii) control environment; (iii) disclosure and transparency; (iv) shareholder rights and (v) stakeholder relations. Some parts of the Code go beyond minimum legal and regulatory requirements, encouraging companies to raise the quality of their governance more in line with international best practices.

In addition to these prescriptions and legislations on corporate governance, Vietnam has seen an increase in training, publications and research and delegations to gather international experience. 2018 saw for example the launch of the VIOD. This influential organization resulted from the productive collaboration between a variety of regulators and private sector representatives under the Vietnam Corporate Governance Initiative. VIOD now plays a crucial role in advancing board professionalism, networking directors and promoting business ethics and transparency in order to support Vietnamese companies to adopt better governance practices. Whilst these efforts have achieved certain positive results, the path of aligning with international corporate governance standards remains challenging in Vietnam.

4.5.1 An Alignment with International Best Practices and Asian Peers in Terms of Corporate Governance Is Overdue

The figure below shows summary data of the Corporate Governance Scorecards, a metric developed by the Asian Development Bank to gauge the quality of corporate governance over time and in selected Asian countries. Vietnam scores lowest and the rate of increase in the period 2012 to 2015 has been less remarkable than in other countries. However, there is much hope that, finally, awareness of good corporate governance, skills and experience of board directors and investor demand for increased transparency and accountability will push Vietnam's corporate governance quality to levels comparable with the best in the region (Fig. 4.7).

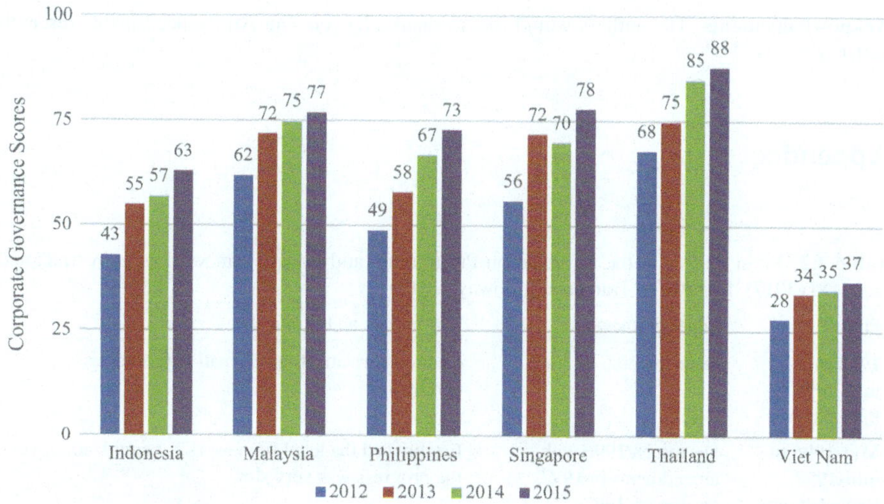

Fig. 4.7 A Comparison of Corporate Governance Scores. *Source* Asian Development Bank (2015)

4.6 Conclusion

The economy of Vietnam is still in transition after twenty years of efforts to increase market forces in the economic allocation process. Coming from a centrally planned economic model, it was only in the late 1990s that the government implemented measures which lie at the heart of this shift: private ownership of productive assets. A mix of ideological barriers, a lack of skills, contradictory economic policies and vested interests have slowed down any progress in this privatization process. It is observed that the government has focused on privatizing smaller enterprises typically owned by provincial, municipal or party authorities. As a result, the percentage contribution of SOEs to overall GDP has steadily but slowly declined throughout the last twenty years. However, large enterprises owned by central government authorities have so far been exempted from passing ownership to private hands. These enterprises represent the next frontier in the drive to reduce further the government's role in the economy. The stakes are high this time: the remaining companies are very visible both nationally and internationally, have national presence and employ hundreds of thousands. Consequently, the government is hard pressed to resort to international best practices in the process and pre- and post-privatization governance of these enterprises.

New institutions like the government's Super Committee and the VIOD coupled with new or improved regulations and legislation like the laws and frameworks for good corporate governance are in place now. With these, Vietnam may, after a prolonged transition process, achieve a more desirable amount of market forces. This ultimately is a stepping stone for the country to secure long-term prosperity and a key role in the world economy.

Acknowledgements The authors would like to thank Nguyen Thu An for her capable research assistance.

Appendix

Table 4.2 Main Phases in the Equitization Programme and Legal Frameworks. *Source* adapted from Do (2017), Le (2017), Tran and Holloway (2014)

Phases	Legal Frameworks	Key Events and Progress
1992 to mid-1996 Pilot phase	Decision 202	Cautious privatization of small unprofitable enterprises
Mid-1996 to mid-1998 Extended pilot phase	Decree 28/1996 with amendments in 1997, Decree 25/1997	Established the legal framework for equitization, yet the progress was very slow
Mid-1998 to 2006 Accelerated phase	Decrees 48/1998/ND-C, 44/1998, 64/2002, 187/2004 Decision 151/2005/QD-TTg, Law on Enterprises (2005), Law on Securities (2006)	**2000**: First stock exchange—Ho Chi Minh City (HCMC) Securities Trading Center (Decree 48/1998) **2005**: established State Capital Investment Corporation (SCIC—Decision 151/2005) and Hanoi Securities Trading Centre (HASTC—Decision 127/1998) Most active period (2003–2006) saw over 2600 SOEs equitized as of the preparation process to accede WTO
2007–2010	Decree 109/2007/QĐ-TTg[a] Decision No. 599/QD-TTg Decision 01/2009/QĐ-TTg	Slowed down after 2007: global crisis, poor performance of Vietnamese stock exchanges, prolonged preparation of large SOEs to-be-equitized **2007**: Ho Chi Minh Stock Exchange (HOSE) replace HCMC Securities Trading Centre (Decision 599/2007) **2009**: Hanoi Stock Exchange (HNX) replaced HASTC (Decision 01/2009); launch of a market for unlisted public companies (UPCoM)
2011–2015 Economic restructuring phase	Decree 59/2011, 189/2013, 116/2015, 81/2015	**2011:** credit crisis (ADB 2015) **2012:** Introduction of the HNX 30 Index – SOEs would be categorised into subcategories in which the state government is 100%, 65% - 50%, and under 50% (Decision 929/2012/QĐ- TTg)
2016–2020 A new wave of equitization	Decree 126/2017/ND-CP; Decision 58/2016 (divestment ratios), 26/2019/QD-TTg, 1232/QĐ-TTg[b]	Stricter requirements for equitized SOEs to become listed companies Voluntary guidelines to adhere to international best practices in corporate governance

[a]Decision on promulgating regulations for building and implementing national investment promotion program for the 2007–2010 period
[b]Decision specifying Corporate Governance Code of Best Practices for Public Companies

References

ADB (2015) State-Owned Enterprise Reform in Viet Nam: Lessons Learnt and Future Directions

Beeson M, Pham HH (2012) Developmentalism with Vietnamese characteristics: the persistence of state-led development in East Asia. J Contemporary Asia 42(4):539–559. https://doi.org/10.1080/00472336.2012.706481

Do H (2017) Privatizing SOEs—implications for foreign investors. KPMG Vietnam Webinar. Hanoi: KPMG Vietnam

Doan NPA, Nguyen DT (2013) Accounting in a developing transitional economy: the case of Vietnam. Asian Rev Account 21(1):74–95. https://doi.org/10.1108/13217341311316959

Fujita M (2017) Vietnamese State-owned Enterprises under International Economic Integration. RIETI Discussion Paper Series

Gainsborough M (2009) Privatisation as state advance: Private indirect government in Vietnam. New Political Economy 14(2):257–274. https://doi.org/10.1080/13563460902826013

GSO (2018) Doanh nghiệp, Hợp tác xã và Cơ sở kinh tế cá thể phi nông nghiệp (Enterprise, Cooperative and Non-farm individual business establishment). In Vietnam Statistical Yearbook 2018 (pp. 287–469). Hanoi: General Statistics Office of Vietnam (GSO)

Ha Thu (2018, May 30) Vietnam to retain three state economic groups by 2020. The Hanoitimes. Ha Noi

Jamieson NL, Osborne ME, Duiker WJ, Buttinger J, Hickey GC, Turley WS (2019) Vietnam | History, Population, Map & Facts. In Encyclopædia Britannica. Encyclopædia Britannica, inc. https://www.britannica.com/place/Vietnam. Accessed 25 November 2019

La Porta R, Lopez-de-Silanes F, Shleifer A, Vishny R (1999) The quality of government. J La, Econ Organ 15(1):222–279. https://doi.org/10.1093/jleo/15.1.222

Le HH (2017, July) Vietnam's New Wave of SOE Equitization : Drivers and Implications. Perspective: Researchers at ISEAS—Yusof Ishak Institute—Analyse Current Events (57):1–8. https://www.iseas.edu.sg/images/pdf/ISEAS_Perspective_2017_57.pdf

Megginson WL, Netter JM (2001) From state to market: a survey of empirical studies on privatization. J Econ Literat 39(2):321–389. https://doi.org/10.1257/jel.39.2.321

Mühlenkamp H (2015) From state to market revisited: a reassessment of the empirical evidence on the efficiency of public (and privately-owned) enterprises. Ann Public Cooperative Econ 86(4):535–557. https://doi.org/10.1111/apce.12092

Ngo VL (1993) reform and rural development: impact on class, sectoral, and regional inequalities. In: Turley WS, Selden M (eds), Reinventing Vietnamese Socialism: Doi Moi in Comparative Perspective. New York: Taylor & Francis. https://doi.org/10.4324/9780429304309-8

Nguyen VT, Freeman NJ (2009) State-owned enterprises in Vietnam: are they "crowding out" the private sector? Post-Communist Economies 21(2):227–247. https://doi.org/10.1080/14631370902778674

Painter M (2008) From command economy to hollow state? decentralisation in Vietnam and China. Australian J Public Administr 67(1):79–88. https://doi.org/10.1111/j.1467-8500.2007.00570.x

Phan D, Joshi M, Tran-Nam B (2018) The history of accounting standard setting in an emerging transition economy: the case of Vietnam. Accounting History 23(3):379–406. https://doi.org/10.1177/1032373217745672

Rama M (2014) Viet Nam. In: Looney RE (ed), Handbook of emerging economies (pp 339–363). New York: Routledge. https://doi.org/10.30875/feecd05f-en

Tran THL, Holloway DA (2014) Developments in corporate governance: the case of Vietnam. Corporate Ownership Control 11(3 C):219–230

Viet Nam News (2018, October 1) 'Super committee' for State-run firms debuts. Viet Nam News. Ha Noi. https://vietnamnews.vn/economy/466862/super-committee-for-state-run-firms-debuts.html#hHXDJXVyuMBIjk8h.97. Accessed 1 October 2019

Zhu Y, Collins N, Webber M, Benson J (2008) New forms of ownership and human resource practices in Vietnam. Human Resour Manag 47(1):157–175. https://doi.org/10.1002/hrm.20202

Chapter 5
Labour and Special Economic Zones

5.1 Introduction

Although the concept of setting aside specific pieces of land to be administered under different forms of low has been pursued for various reasons throughout history, the popularity of the special economic zone (SEZ)[1] really took off when the Chinese government demonstrated that it was possible to use them as a means of raising hundreds of millions of people out of poverty without making any concessions to political plurality. This was an initiative that was to prove compelling to governments across Asia and beyond so that there is now scarcely a country in the world which does not have its own complement. More than 75% of all countries host zones of some sort and there is a global total now in excess of 4,800 (World Investment Forum 2018). Even North Korea has a border SEZ with South Korea at Kaesong, where the North provides the labour and the South provides everything else, albeit that it is closed more often than open (Walsh 2014).

The SEZs used in China were different in size but not in nature from the export-processing zones (EPZs) created after World War II to help rebuild European economies. The EPZs were located near sea or airports and were intended to be isolated from the rest of the country—customarily, they were walled off from the outside world and guarded by security officers. They promoted exports by providing a physical space in which customs duties were not payable. It was understood that the first goal of economic development (i.e. moving from low income to middle

[1] The term special economic zone (SEZ) is used in this chapter as any piece of land that has been separated in time and space from neighbouring areas and made subject to different laws and regulations. Customarily, the changes in law benefit capital at the expense of labour and these changes are used to encourage greater flows of domestic and foreign direct investment (FDI) into specific geographic areas so as to promote specific developmental goals for those areas. The term SEZ in Vietnam refers to one specific type of zone, which is a subset of all SEZs considered in the chapter.

J. Walsh et al., *The Political Economy of Vietnam's Industrial Transformation*,
SpringerBriefs in Political Science,
https://doi.org/10.1007/978-981-16-0151-4_5

income status) was import substitution but countries entering the manufacturing era generally operated with an excess of supply over demand for labour that keeps labour costs low and means workers generally cannot buy the products they help to make. As a result, manufacturing was aimed at export promotion in the first stage. It is when the Lewisian point of the equalisation of demand and supply of labour in the manufacturing sector is reached that the policy focus switches from export orientation to import substitution.

Jacobs (1985) observed that the second stage of economic development, during which a country can move from medium income to high income status, involves the promotion of innovation, not just in manufacturing but in all sectors of the economy. However, innovation linked to manufacturing is likely to remain of crucial importance, as the modern histories of Germany and Japan attest. She further argued that successful innovation requires an assemblage of skills, infrastructure, supply and demand factors that can only be provided by a city and a relatively well-connected city at that. However, cities may not always be conveniently located for a variety of reasons and states may prefer, in effect, to create their own cities by establishing SEZs of such scope and sophistication that they perform the functions of a city that are required for innovation to have a chance to flourish (see Tables 5.1 and 5.2). This has led the World Bank (2017:11) to move towards a definition of SEZs such that they occupy geofigureically delimited areas, contain multiple companies, have a zone management facility or administration and have a government land policy.

A new generation of SEZs has emerged, therefore, which are far from isolated from the rest of the economy but, in fact, connected and even hyper-connected with it. In Lao PDR, for example, a series of special and specific economic zones has been designed to serve a series of different purposes and characteristically include schools, hospitals, residential areas, restaurants, sporting and leisure facilities such that executives, specifically foreign executives, will be willing to relocate there. In Cambodia, on the other hand, strategically important economic activities have been identified and, if these are to be performed, the companies involved will automatically receive the benefits of being located within an SEZ. In Vietnam, developments

Table 5.1 The connectivity matrix. *Source* Walsh (2013)

	Internal	External
Physical	Facilities (buildings, plant, pollution)	Common infrastructure (transportation, utilities, sewerage etc.)
Virtual	Websites, networks	Internet
Commercial	Marketing and PR	Business development services (e.g. business matching, networking, structured learning opportunities)
Organizational	Cross-border intra-firm exchanges	Industrial Estate authority initiatives
Personal	Friends, personal relationships	Religious groups, hobby groups, civil society

Table 5.2 Characteristics of Industrial Estates and Special Economic Zones. *Source* Author

	Industrial estates	Special economic zones
Basis of competitiveness	Low cost competitiveness, economies of scope and scale	Product feature and branding competitiveness, economy of scope and learning
Relationship to economy overall	Standalone production site, island	Connected to multiple nodes of production and consumption, archipelago
Relationship to local economy	Isolated from local economy	Connected in multiple ways to local economy through R&D and university linkages, creating supply chains and clusters
Human resources strategy	Often antagonistic workplace relations	Fostering creativity, diversity and inclusivity in the workplace
Relationship to the environment	Enforced compliance with environmental standards	Aiming to contribute to better environmental conditions
Relationship to infrastructure	Working in addition to existing infrastructure	Designed to be part of smart infrastructure networks and systems

in SEZs have tended to focus on diversification of purpose and governance. An example of this is in the development of seven technology parks (TPs) throughout the country as an attempt to help improve the quality of human resources who can join international companies investing in Vietnam. Of these, Quang Trung Software Park (QTSP) was originally established by government order in 2000 and came into operation the following year, based in the southern capital of Ho Chi Minh City. The city has a long colonial past and has maintained some links with international investors as a result. Its first designation was Quang Trung Software City and it offered the following competitive advantages:

- Space, location and growth;
- Excellent network infrastructure;
- Complex functions;
- High quality services, but low cost (QTSP 2011).

QTSC was successful and became Vietnam's largest software park and attracted investment from the USA, Japan, Korea and Germany, among others. Companies investing there included HP, IBM, GHP Far East, Digi-TEXX, Luxsoft and TUV Rheinland. ISO 9001 was also achieved by the managers, QTSC Development Company (Trinh et al. 2013). It was seen as a model that could be replicated in Ho Chi Minh City and also in other parts of the country (Vietnam.net 2014). Nevertheless, it faces some problems with supply of qualified employees, since now only about 20% of qualified employees are available each year (Walsh 2019).

Of course, building and managing SEZs does have negative aspects. In some countries, most notably in India, it has become associated with land-grabbing and the forced removal of people from the land with which they are familiar. Second,

- Tax holidays or reduced effective tax rates for a specified period;
- Reduction or removal of import duties;
- Changed conditions for freedom of association and collective bargaining by workers;
- Ability to network with other companies in the same zone;
- Ability to conduct high-level dialogue with government;
- Government support for domestic SMEs to enable them better to link with investing companies.

Fig. 5.1 Typical Incentives to Invest in a SEZ. *Source* author

in order to encourage inward FDI, some governments have restricted the rights of the working people involved to such an extent that exploitation has taken place. For example, the story of Foxconn's factories in China has become well-known, while garment factories in Cambodia are known for mass fainting incidents by women workers and the harsh treatment of workers demonstrating for better pay or working conditions. Third, during the period in which Thailand's government was planning to open up to 19 border SEZs, it became evident that insufficient attention has been paid to stress on water supplies and the local environment. In addition to these issues, it is also the case that SEZs will not automatically be successful, especially when the zones are built because of top-down government fiat rather than in response to genuine demand for their presence. Indeed, the World Bank (2017:5) has concluded that the performance of SEZs is quite closely linked to overall national performance, that SEZ performance is difficult to sustain over time and that most incentives and programs (see Fig. 5.1) make little real difference to firm performance.

The developmental purposes of SEZs may be summarised as follows:

– Overall increase in economic activities;
– Increase in economic activities in specific areas or sectors;
– Integrate local economic activities more closely with international of global activities and
– To conduct policy experiments bounded in place and time.

Vietnam has certainly grasped the opportunity to use SEZs in all of these aspects. The government has designed a quite complex regional development plan based on several levels of industrial organization, starting with the four key economic regions (KER) concept (Tables 5.3 and 5.4).

In addition to these zones, there are also industrial parks, with 64 in the Northern KER, 45 in the Central KER, 150 in the Southern KER and 47 in the Mekong KER (VIIPIP n.d.). These parks tend to be non-specific in their purpose and to have been created and operated by a variety of partnerships of development agencies. Their size and degree of infrastructure also varies.

Table 5.3 Key Economic Regions. *Source* adapted from Dezan Shira and Associates (2017)

Name	Provinces	Purpose
Northern KER	Hanoi, Bac Ninh, Hai Duong, Hai Phong	Proximity to Hanoi and China +1 strategy
Central KER	Da Nang, Quang Nam, Quang Ngai, Binh Dinh	Infrastructure, seafood
Mekong KER	An Giang, Ca Mau, Can Tho, Kien Giang	Thailand +1 strategy
Southern KER	Binh Duong, Binh Phuc, Long An, Ho Chi Minh City, Tay Ninh, Dong Nai	Proximity to Ho Chi Minh City and labour force

Table 5.4 Variety of Development Zones in Vietnam. *Source* adapted from Dezan Shire and Associates (2013)

Name	Benefit
Industrial zones (IZs)	Specialise in support for and manufacture of industrial products. Additional incentives may be provided for areas with difficult economic conditions
Economic zones (EZs)	Offer additional incentives to individuals and companies when located in especially difficult socio-economic conditions
Export processing zones (EPZs)	Specialise in manufacturing products for export and are tariff-free as a result
High-tech zones (HTZs)	Promote high-tech manufacturing such as biotechnology, green technology and IT, as well as training employees and research and development (R&D) activities. Similar incentives exist as for EZs
	Note: this range of zones varies in specific terms and conditions on a case-by-case basis. The determination of these is often delegated to local authority bodies, which can exercise some discretion with an overall national framework

5.2 SEZs in Vietnam

Since 1986, when the Vietnamese government adopted the *Đổi Mới* policy to restructure its command economy to become a market-oriented one, it has used numerous SEZs as hosts for inwards foreign direct investment (FDI). There are 292 IPs, 3 EPZs and 15 economic zones (EZs), with others planned. An EZ is defined as a "… zone which has an economic area separated from the investment and business environment with geographical boundaries and especially favourable conditions for investors and established in accordance with the regulations of the government in the Decree No. 29/2008/ND-CP (MPI 2009)." Although these are located throughout the country, most SEZs are concentrated in the vicinities of Hanoi's Red River Basin and Ho Chi Minh City. There are also 18 border gate zones, as described below.

Actual details of how SEZs are managed may be delegated to the provincial level. For example, the Da Nang City Party Cell Congress announced various targets, including the wish to make the city an important socioeconomic sector of the country "... playing the role of a service centre, a seaport city, an important traffic hub for national and international transhipment, a centre for post-telecommunications, finance and banking, a centre for health, culture, sports, education, training, science, technology, a centre for training high quality human resources," among other goals (Vietnam Trade Promotion Agency 2013). To achieve these goals, six major IPs have been opened, which are Da Nang IP, Hoa Khanh IP, Hoa Khanh IP Expansion, Lien Chieu IP, Hoa Cam IP and Da Nang Seafood Service Industrial Zone. The city was also soliciting investment in the Da Nang High Technology Park and the Concentrated Information Technology Park.

However, the SEZs in Vietnam to date, although they are said to employ more than 2.2 million people, have not been uniformly successful owing to unclear administrative processes, excess of supply over demand regionally as well as nationally and a lack of a clear strategy embodied in a law. For example, the Vung Tau-Con Dao SEZ was created in 1979 and then dissolved in 1991, apparently because of poor performance. Nevertheless, a policy on SEZ construction was added to the constitution in 1992 and this was strengthened by a Resolution passed by the Party Central Committee in 1994 (Vong 2016).

At the end of 2016, the government announced a policy to launch three new SEZs with new economic and administrative policies, which will be trialled there first with a view to subsequently introducing them to the remainder of the country. These zones will be in Van Don (Quang Ninh province), Van Phong (Khanh Hoa province) and Phu Quoc Island (Kien Giang province). It is not yet clear how these SEZs will be administered.

Vietnam's border gates (see below) are considered to be potential or actual tourist destinations where people can shop at kiosks from both sides of the border (the Vietnamese traders use characteristically large cargo bicycles). The Lao Cai border gate with China is going to be developed into an EZ that will drive development in the area. As much as 15,929.8 hectares of land will be involved and this incorporate three precincts, 24 communes and one town with 89 hamlets in Lao Cai city, together with four other districts. A comprehensive vision for the areas unites sustainable urban and economic development with security and national sovereignty (Vietnam Breaking News 2017) (Table 5.5).

The city of Hekou lies over the Chinese side of the border line. The gate was closed after the Sino-Vietnamese War of 1979 but then opened again in 1993. Trade through the gate reached US$254 million in the first three months of 2017, which is a more than 10% increase of the fourth quarter of 2016. Goods exported from Vietnam included iron ore, footwear, agricultural products, confectionery and milk, while goods imported into China included agricultural products, fertilisers, chemicals, steel, machinery and other products. Customs procedures at the border have been streamlined (Vietnam Breaking News 2017).

There is support for cross-border economic zones (CBEZs) from the Chinese side. Despite having a land border 22,000 km long, only 5% of trade for China comes in

Table 5.5 Vietnam's Border Gates. *Source* adapted by the author from various sources

Neighbouring Country	Gate	Province
China	Lao Cai	Lao Cai
	Mong Cai	Quang Ninh
	Huu Nghi	Lang Son
	Dong Dang	Lang Son
Lao PDR	Na Meo	Thanh Hoa
	Nam Can	Nghe An
	Keo Nua	Ha Tinh
	Lao Bao	Quang Tri
	Cha Lo	Quang Binh
	Po Y	Kon Tum
	Tay Trang	Dien Bien
Cambodia	Le Thanh	Gia Lai
	Moc Bai	Tay Ninh
	Sa Mat	Tay Ninh
	Dinh Ba	Dong Thap
	Tinh Bien	An Giang
	Xa Xia	Kien Giang
	Vinh Xuong	An Giang

the form of border trade. To improve the situation, the Chinese government has established border economic zones (BEZs) facing a number of neighbours and five of these are with CLMTV countries: Hekou, Pinxiang and Dongxing BEZs neighbour Vietnam; Mohan neighbours Lao PDR and Ruili BEZ neighbours Myanmar. However, border trade across the region was effectively stopped by the outbreak of the coronavirus pandemic. Subsequently, precautions put in place to try to prevent infection have significantly hampered trade and Vietnamese agricultural exports have suffered accordingly.

5.2.1 Attitudes Towards SEZs

Although there are examples of failures with planned SEZ projects, most commonly as a result of lack of demand in a top-down mandated project, most iterations find little difficulty in filling the ranks of workers. Irrespective of the appearance of exploitation of workers in intensive manufacturing, there are still large numbers of people in the world, including Vietnam, who are quite content to exchange factory life for a life on the farm. This does not mean that labour relations within SEZs are always harmonious and there has been dissent or resistance arising from two sources. The first is in the workplace, where, for example, there has been a history of workplace disagreements with, particularly, Korean investors (Byun and Walsh 1998). However, this has resulted in a flexible and sophisticated approach from the Vietnamese General Confederation of Labour (VGCL), which has created a space for progressive discourse for labour rights issues that has been helpful in promoting mediation (Tran 2007b). In general, the government has taken a pro-investment stance which, in common with most if not all countries where this development paradigm has been followed, tends to indicate an anti-worker legal regime (Tran 2007a). Nevertheless, research indicates that industrial action is more common in SEZs than outside them, at least partly because well-organized unions are more likely to be present there, although that does not mean that they are necessarily more efficient in resolving issues (Anner and Liu 2016). In any case, the Vietnamese government has taken care to fulfil its obligations to the tripartite arrangements required by the International Labour Organization (ILO), which are generally accepted around the world.

The second source of dissent has resulted from resistance to inwards investment arising either because of environmental issues or because of resentment of the actions or intentions of the foreign investor. Since such instances of resistance apparently contradict the government's stated policy with respect to inwards investment, these are treated as being sensitive in nature and are little covered in the local media. One estimate of inwards investment suggested that, especially in industries such as leather, almost half of such incidents result in environmental pollution (Truong 2015). These events are sometimes greeted with local complaints but these are generally suppressed quite quickly. Perhaps more problematic are protests against foreign investors for political reasons, since these can very swiftly escalate on a wave of public emotion and become international incidents. The prime example of this is in the case of China, when the Chinese government is being accused of provocations in the South China Sea (known in Vietnam as the Biển Đông or East Sea). This has led to periodic protests but these took a new turn in 2018 when protests became linked to the new SEZ policy which permitted land leasing on a 99-year basis, which some interpreted as meaning that Chinese interests were seizing local land (Elmer 2018). The threat of large-scale protests is considered to be a serious threat to security and government agencies have been willing to make concessions in order to preserve the peace. It is clear that running a complex, contemporary economy requires balancing multiple interests and perspectives that pose specific challenges to the single-party regime compared to the pluralistic state. However, it is not obvious that the dangers posed thereby are necessarily worse or more extreme.

5.2.2 Gender Aspects

The move from agriculture to manufacturing involves the movement of both men and women away from the countryside to the factory. In the case of male migration, this can contribute to the greying of agriculture as older farmers tend to stay on the farms they know, while younger farmers may be more willing to try new forms of income generation. In the case of women, although the basic dynamic remains the same, the actual results are far more complex and the effects more far-reaching. Women who move from agricultural households to factories tend to move from being unwaged providers of emotional and domestic labour to waged earners working in a capitalist system. Instead of providing personal care for their family members, perhaps including children, they are instead mostly absent from the home but can contribute to providing consumer goods for family care or contribute to paying for healthcare or education (Hui 1996:5–9). Irrespective of how the money is spent, the relationship between the women and their families is significantly changed and it may not be possible to return to the previous situation. Although no crossing of borders has taken place, the situation is quite similar to international labour migration in that the changes experienced by the workers concerned can be of such significance that their life view changes and, concomitantly, their willingness to cede the agency they have obtained over their lives is attenuated.

Observation of similar situations reveals that women have opportunities, through living in dormitories or other forms of employer-provided accommodation, to establish personal relationships that they would not have been able to establish if they had remained on the farm (Michinobu 2005:27–9). Of course, these relationships are not necessarily entirely positive ones and there are risks of unwanted pregnancies, sexually transmitted diseases and other issues. However, it would be wrong to assume that the women involved are uniformly naïve and unable to cope with the outside world. Research shows that many if not most women with agency over their movements are able to negotiate the issues involved in dealing with a new environment in all its complexity on their own terms (Hoang and Yeoh 2015). Even so, there are examples of women with lower levels of education who may be able to earn money but may not be given decision-making power over what to do with that money (Viet Nam News 2016). In the case of women from ethnic minority backgrounds, particularly when they are based in comparatively remote areas, there may be a need for consciousness-raising and information provision campaigns for the women to be able to realise the opportunities that are available to them (Phuong 2012).

5.2.3 Trade Unions

Trade unionism has quite an extensive history in Vietnam and was first established in 1929 at the Tonkin Red Federation of Trade Unions under the supervision of the Communist Party of Vietnam (Nhan Dan 2019). The Vietnam Trade Union (VTU) thus formed has subsequently been transformed into the Vietnam General Confederation of Labour (VGCL). According to its Charter, the VGCL has a number of functions in its mandate to be loyal to the interests of the working class and developing peace, democracy, national independence, development and social progress, including: "… to represent and protect workers' legitimate and legal rights and interests, to participate in state management, socio-economic management and in the inspection, examination, monitoring of activities of state agencies, organizations, establishments, enterprises, to propagate, encourage workers to study, improve qualification, professional skill, to observe laws and to build and defend the socialist Fatherland of Vietnam (11th Vietnam Trades Union Congress n.d.)".

Research indicates that the union effectively fulfils its basic function of representing the interests of workers and providing them with better terms and conditions in the workplace (Torm 2014). Promotion of bilateral relations with unions in other countries has been used in order to maintain the interests of both sides, which is particularly important in the case of Korea, owing to the extensive Korean investments in Vietnam (Vietnam Plus 2019). From 2018, an initiative emerged to join unions in 48 cities across different zones in the country known as the IZ Trade Unions Network, which would facilitate union activities working on a voluntary basis and uniting the VGCL and the ILO's New Industrial Relations Framework, which is supported in part by the Japanese government (ILO 2018). Even so, recent years have seen an increase in industrial action, including wildcat strikes, which have gone mostly unreported in the state-controlled local media. This might have prompted the opportunity to create independent unions, which was announced at a time when minimum wage growth had decreased and uncertainty over the future economic model of the country was becoming evident (Hutt 2019). The signing of a free trade agreement with the EU seemed to indicate that more mileage could be obtained from the low labour cost intensive manufacturing model, without moving to rebalance the economy by enhancing domestic demand. However, there is a countervailing force revealed by the coronavirus pandemic, which demonstrated the suddenly fragile nature of transboundary supply and value chains and the concomitant movement towards deglobalisation. However these forces settle into a new pattern, workers will wish to have a voice heard and this may lead to further concessions being made in future years.

5.3 Vietnam's Labour Market

The labour market in Vietnam is more than 53 million in total, which is certainly above average for the range of all countries in the world. A larger workforce tends to indicate that it will take longer to incorporate all agricultural workers into the manufacturing sector and so the period of time during which low labour cost competitiveness can be used will also tend to be a little longer. The act of encouraging inwards investment in a country with a view to establishing export-oriented manufacturing factories leads to internal migration, as workers move from rural areas to predominantly urban ones, which in turn leads to urbanization and the challenges this poses for residential accommodation, water management, public health and the provision of government services to support growing communities. Change also arises in the area of gender relations as women enter the waged workforce for the first time and move from being unpaid providers of domestic and emotional labour to recipients of wages that make them consumers living independently and with some additional agency over their personal lives (Table 5.6).

Table 5.6 Vietnam: Employed Population Aged 15 and Over by Sex, Urban/Rural and Economic Sector (Q4, 2016) (000 s Persons). *Source* adapted from MPI General Statistical Office, Report on Labour Force Survey, Quarter 4, 2016 (Hanoi: GSO 2016), p. 26, Table 5.7

	Total	Male	Female
Whole Country	53,405.4	27,528.6	25,876.8
State Sector	5,150.7	2,648.6	2,502.1
Non-state Sector	45,818.5	24,056.3	21,762.2
Foreign Investment	2,431.7	822.3	1,609.4
Not Stated	4.5	1.3	3.2
Urban	17,006.8	8,781.7	8,225.1
State Sector	2,988.7	1,556.6	1,432.1
Non-state Sector	12,979.0	6,841.7	6,137.3
Foreign Investment	1,036.8	382.2	654.6
Not Stated	2.4	1.2	1.1
Rural	36,398.5	18,746.9	17,651.7
State Sector	2,161.9	1,092.0	1,070.7
Non-state Sector	32,839.5	17,214.7	15,624.9
Foreign Investment	1,394.9	440.1	954.8
Not Stated	2.1	0.1	2.1

Vietnam's labour productivity has been increasing in recent years, albeit from quite a low base. Figures by the General Statistical Office (GSO) showed that Singapore workers were 13.7 times more productive than Vietnamese ones, Malaysian workers 5.3 times, Thai workers 2.7 times and Indonesian workers 2.2 times more productive (Viet Nam News 2019). However, labour productivity has risen by 22.5% since 2008 and is now estimated to be valued at VND 93.2 million (YS$4,139) per annum (Dezan Shira and Associates 2018). Productivity is not increasing as quickly as wage growth and particular problems remain in the agriculture and agroforestry sectors, which are among those where there are issues relating to outdated machinery, limited workforce quality and poor management of resources (Viet Nam News 2019).

The minimum wage rate in Vietnam varies from region to region, in part reflecting differences in types of economic activity which occur in different parts of the country and, also, recognising different costs of living that apply.

There are problems with the structure of the workforce, with a bias among the population as a whole (and particularly among the urban middle classes) against vocational education meaning that there tends to be a shortage of skilled and semi-skilled workers in the emergent markets that would enable Vietnamese SMEs to participate profitably from joining supply chains organized by inward investing firms (Tables 5.7 and 5.8).

The fact that Vietnam's workforce is not well-placed to move towards industry 4.0 activities is demonstrated by the low level of importance placed on the creative industries in the country. Whereas internationally the creative industries might represent 10% of GDP (and hence create some US$592 billion in earnings), in Vietnam it is restricted to just 5–10% (British Business Group Vietnam 2019). Following

Table 5.7 Minimum Wage Rates in Vietnam, 2019. *Source* Dezan Shira and Associates (2019)

Region	Minimum Monthly Wage Rate 2019	Change on 2018
1: Hanoi and Ho Chi Minh City	VND 4,180,000 (US$180)	+200,000
2: Urban Can Tho, Da Nang and Hai Phong	VND 3,710,000 (US$159)	+180,000
3: Provincial cities and districts of Bac Ninh, Bac Giang, Hai Duong and Vinh Phuc	VND 3,250,000 (US$140)	+160,000
4: Remainder of the country	VND 2,920,000 (US$125)	+160,000

Table 5.8 Skilled Workers in Vietnam, 2011–3. *Source* GSO Quarterly labour and employment survey (2012, 2013)

	2011	2012	2013
Number of technical skilled workers (millions)	23.9	24.6	25.5
Proportion of technical skilled workers (%)	45.2	46.0	47.4
Technical workers without degree/certificate	27.9	28.0	29.0
Workers with degree/certificate	17.3	18.0	18.4
Vocational trained workers	5.2	5.3	5.3

UNCTAD guidelines, 15 sectors have been designated as creative industries in Vietnam, which are: designing and prototyping; graphic design; advertising and marketing; communications; newspapers and publishing; digital content; handicrafts; fashion design; art performance; music; game and software design; cinema and television; architecture; culinary arts; and creative consulting. The government has been working with universities to help support these activities. For example, RMIT Vietnam is introducing undergraduate level courses and majors in fashion management and digital applications for business. Nevertheless, there remains a current and a future shortage in skills that will need to be addressed if Vietnam is to upgrade its current economic model.

5.4 Conclusion

The SEZ-based intensive manufacturing paradigm has proved to be popular throughout the rapidly developing economies of Southeast Asia. It has been embraced more thoroughly by the Vietnamese government than any other. SEZs in Vietnam, using a broad category that encompasses all the different forms of spatial economic initiatives employed in the country, are present in the largest numbers and are more likely to be governed by local governmental authorities and to be used in part as sites for policy experiments. This has been a feature of modern economic policy in the country: "Determination, unity, and willingness to experiment and recognize failure within the country's leadership came to play a critical role in Viet Nam's subsequent economic history and development process (Tarp 2018)." As a result, different portions of its territory are marked out for selective relaxation of various laws and regulations, while incentives to invest may be put into place in time-limited projects which are likely to have specific state-level or regional developmental goals with respect to industrialisation. In line with the contemporary conceptualisation of SEZs that they can be used to resemble cities or provide city-like effects in locations considered convenient by government actors, these zones can now incorporate health, educational, retail and leisure facilities in addition to the more common factories, warehouses and transportation depots. This makes zones more attractive to foreign investors concerned that the local economy cannot provide desired facilities and services at desirable prices. It keeps zones further from integration with the local economy and this might be attractive to policy-makers who might prefer investors to keep their opinions of local politics to themselves.

In order to support SEZs aiming to serve so many different purposes, it is necessary to train or otherwise produce workers equipped with the requisite skills and competencies and this has proved to be something of a strain. Although efforts have been taken to produce more qualified workers with advanced skills likely to be needed in the future, in the absence of a full-scale labour market planning system, there is always likely to be a mismatch between supply and demand for skilled and semi-skilled workers, especially in a country as large as Vietnam. There is scope for the introduction of more computerized systems matching desired skills and available positions on a more timely basis.

Economic zones are popular for foreign investors and their facilities, together with improvements in transportation infrastructure assisted by the ADB's Asian Highway Network and Chinese investment will, eventually, help to eliminate the regional variations in Vietnam's labour market and this will help to encourage higher quality investment as employers will have more incentive to provide more skills to the workers they have rather than relying on finding those who will work for low wages. In turn, this will help to regularise the country's still extensive informal sector as more opportunities will arise in the expanding formal sector.

References

11th Vietnam Trades Union Congress (n.d.) Charter of Vietnam Trades Unions. ILO. https://www.ilo.org/dyn/natlex/docs/MONOGRAPH/94503/128468/F448597516/VNM94503%20Eng2.pdf

Anner M, Liu X (2016) Harmonious union and rebellious workers: a study of wildcat strikes in Vietnam. ILR Rev 69(1):3–28

British Business Group Vietnam (BBGV) (2019) Vietnam market briefing: Creative industry. https://bbgv.org/wp-content/uploads/2017/10/Creative-industry-in-Vietnam.pdf

Byun H-Y, Walsh J (1998) Strategic investment policy in South-East Asia: Korean firms in Vietnam. Pacific Focus 13(1):99–123

Dezan Shira and Associates, "Development Zones in Vietnam" (June 4th, 2013), available at: https://www.vietnam-briefing.com/news/development-zones-vietnam.html

Dezan Shira and Associates (2017) Vietnam's key regions and economic zones, Vietnam Briefing 31. https://www.iberglobal.com/files/2017-2/vietnam-key-regions-economic-zones.pdf

Dezan Shira and Associates (2018) Labour market trends in Vietnam. https://www.vietnam-briefing.com/news/labour-market-trends-vietnam.html/

Dezan Shira and Associates (2019) Vietnam hikes minimum wages by 5.3 percent in 2019. https://www.vietnam-briefing.com/news/vietnam-hikes-minimum-wages-by-5-3-percent-in-2019.html/

Elmer K (2018, June 13) Anti-Chinese protests in Vietnam set to aggravate tensions with Beijing. South China Morning Post. https://www.scmp.com/news/china/diplomacy-defence/article/2150653/anti-china-protests-vietnam-set-aggravate-tensions

General Statistical Office (GSO) (2016) Report on labour force survey, quarter 4, 2016. (Hanoi: GSO

GSO (2012, 2013) Quarterly labour and employment survey. http://khcn.molisa.gov.vn/books/thị trườnglaođộng.pdf

Hoang LA, Yeoh BSA (2015) 'I'd do it for love or for money: Vietnamese women in Taiwan and the social construction of female migrant sexuality. Gender Place Culture 22(5):591–607

Hui AWS (1996) Assembling gender: the making of the Malay female labour. Strategic Info Research Development, Petaling Jaya

Hutt D (2019) Workers of Vietnam, unite? The Diplomat. https://thediplomat.com/2019/11/workers-of-vietnam-unite/

International Labour Organization (ILO) (2018) Nation's industrial zone unions network established. https://www.ilo.org/hanoi/Informationresources/Publicinformation/newsitems/WCMS_635347/lang--en/index.htm

Jacobs J (1985) Cities and the wealth of nations: Principles of economic life. Random House Publishing USA, New York, NY

Michinobu R (2005) Lives in transition: the influence of Northern Thailand's economic and cultural change on young factory women's sexual behavior and HIV risk. Centre for Health Policy Studies, Nakhon Pathom

MPI (2009) United Nations Industrial Development Organization Country Office in Vietnam (2015) Economic zones in the ASEAN: Industrial parks, special economic zones, eco industrial parks, innovation districts as strategies for industrial competitiveness. Hanoi: UNIDO

Nhan Dan (2019, July 28) Vietnam trade union promotes its tradition to contribute to national renewal. https://en.nhandan.com.vn/politics/domestic/item/7742102-vietnam-trade-union-promotes-its-tradition-to-contribute-to-national-renewal.html

Phuong PQ (2012) Gender, empowerment and development: Gender relations from the perspective of ethnic minorities in Vietnam, Institute of Social Studies, Economics and Environment. https://isee.org.vn/wp-content/uploads/2018/11/gender-empowerment-and-development-gender-relations-from-the-perspective-of-ethnic-minorities-in-vietnam.pdf

Quang Trung Software Park (QTSP) (2011) Who we are. https://web.archive.org/web/20110501200030/ http://www.quangtrungsoft.com.vn:80/index.php/en/about-qtsc/who-we-are?start=3

Tarp F (2018) Viet Nam: the dragon that rose from the ashes, United Nations University (UNU)-WIDER Working Paper 2018/126. https://www.wider.unu.edu/sites/default/files/Publications/working-paper/PDF/wp2018.126.pdf

Torm N (2014) The role of trade unions in Vietnam: a case study of small and medium enterprises. J Int Dev 26(2):207–211

Tran AN (2007a) Alternatives to the 'race to the bottom' in Vietnam: Minimum wage strikes and their aftermath. Labour Stud J 32(4):430–451

Tran AN (2007b) The third sleeve: emerging labour newspapers and the response of the labour unions and the state to workers' resistance in Vietnam. Labour Studies J 32(3):257–279

Trinh VTT, Sriratanaviriyakul N, Nkhoma M, Pham H (2013) Quang Trung Software City—the largest Vietnamese software park. J Inform Technol Educ: Discussion Cases 2(6). https://www.jite.org/documents/DCVol02/v02-06-QuangTrung.pdf

Truong DD (2015) Environmental management in foreign direct investment (FDI) enterprises in Vietnam. Tap chi Khoa hoc Dai hoc Quoc gia Ha Noi 31(5):46–55

Vietnam Breaking News (2017, May 5) Lao Cai border gate EZ to be developed into key economic Area. https://www.vietnambreakingnews.com/2017/05/lao-cai-border-ez-to-be-developed-into-key-economic-area

Vietnam.net (2014, November 13) More software parks to go up. https://english.vietnamnet.vn/fms/science-it/116286/more-software-parks-to-go-up.html

Viet Nam News (2016, March 7) Role of Vietnamese women changing. https://vietnamnews.vn/opinion/in-the-spotligh/283270/role-of-vietnamese-women-changing.html

Viet Nam News (2019, August 8) PM launches labour productivity movement, 2

Vietnam Plus (2019), September 30) Vietnam, RoK enhance trade union cooperation. https://en.vietnamplus.vn/Vietnam-rok-enhance-trade-union-cooperation/160687.vnp

Vietnam Trade Promotion Agency (2013) Fields of investment incentive into Danang and the industrial parks, high technology parks calling for investment of Danang City. http://www.vietrade.gov.vn/en/index.php?option=com_content&view=article&id=2077:fields-of-investment-incentive-into-da-nang-and-the-industrial-parks-high-technology-parks-calling-for-investment-of-danang-city&catid=272:investment-opportunities&Itemid=250

VIIPIP (n.d.). VIIPIP Properties.(n.d.) viipip.com/home/en/

Vong, L.H. (2016, December 20) Gov't oks three special economic Zones, Viet Nam News. http://vietnamnews.vn/economy/business-beat/347650/govt-oks-three-special-economic-zones.html

Walsh J (2013) Social policy and special economic zones in the Greater Mekong Subregion. Int J Soc Quality 3(1):44–56. https://doi.org/10.3167/IJSQ.2013.030104

Walsh J (2014) Joint operation of a special economic zone by enemies: The case of Kaesong Industrial Complex. Int J Nepalese Acad Mana 2(1):80–92. http://www.nam.org.np/userfiles/IJHRM%202014.pdf

Walsh J (2019) Responsible investment issues in special economic zone investment in mainland Southeast Asia. VNU J Sci: Econ Bus 35(2):23–40. https://doi.org/10.25073/2588-1108/vnueab.4226

World Bank (2017) Special economic zones: an operational review of their impacts. Washington, DC: World Bank http://documents.worldbank.org/curated/en/316931512640011812/pdf/P154708-12-07-2017-1512640006382.pdf

World Investment Forum (2018) Special economic zones: Challenges and opportunities. https://worldinvestmentforum.unctad.org/session/free-special-economic-zones-challenges-and-opportunities/

Chapter 6
Vietnamese Political Economy in an East Asian and International Perspective

6.1 Introduction

This chapter provides a comparative overview of Vietnam's socio-economic achievements relative to its Southeast Asian neighbours and the world using data published by the World Bank and others. It will explain the recent acceleration of economic growth and trade, the impact of a fast-aging society and the prevalence of corruption in Vietnam. While reforms of political structures have been timid at best, the reforms of the economic system have been fundamental, as discussed in previous chapters. The outcome of these economic reforms has been so dramatic that the World Bank already in 2008 credited them as "one of the most spectacular success stories in economic development."

This chapter provides answers to the questions where does Vietnam stand today in terms of socio-economic development? Economic growth has been sustained over the last three decades but how does it compare to peers in the regions? Why does corruption persist and what are the consequences for Vietnam's growth agenda? This chapter concludes by shedding light on the challenges ahead, such as the lack of a productive domestic private sector and the persistence of corruption at high levels.

Embedding Vietnam's socio-economic development in the context of the Southeast Asian Region is a useful exercise as countries in this region exhibit strong ties through trade, cross-border investments and a unifying vision of the ASEAN Economic Community. Southeast Asia consists of eleven countries that reach from eastern India to China and is generally divided into mainland and maritime or island zones. The mainland (Myanmar, Thailand, Lao PDR, Cambodia and Vietnam) is an extension of the Asian continent. Island or maritime Southeast Asia includes

J. Walsh et al., *The Political Economy of Vietnam's Industrial Transformation*,
SpringerBriefs in Political Science,
https://doi.org/10.1007/978-981-16-0151-4_6

Malaysia, Singapore, Indonesia, the Philippines, Brunei and the new nation of East Timor (formerly part of Indonesia).[1]

Despite sharing many similarities in climate and biodiversity, these countries feature a diverse range of languages, cultures and religions. In terms of languages, of the six thousand languages spoken in the world today, some one thousand are estimated to be found in Southeast Asia. Linguistically, the mainland is divided into three important families, the Austro-Asiatic (like Cambodian and Vietnamese), Tai (like Thai and Lao) and the Tibeto-Burmese (including highland languages as well as Burmese). Culturally, the region has been influenced by two great civilizations of India and China since the ancient time of maritime trading. Indian-rooted religions such as Hinduism and Buddhism as well as Islam have diffused into the local life of most Southeast Asian countries. Meanwhile, Vietnam, due to its proximity with and long colonization by China in the past, was influenced by ancient Chinese philosophy like Confucianism, Taoism as well as the Mahayana branch of Buddhism, which reached Vietnam via China. Theravadin Buddhism, as practised in the rest of mainland Southeast Asia, arrived via sea from India and Sri Lanka. Still today, the wide spectrum of historic cultural influences is marking the region and that is not to mention the multivalent and powerful indigenous cultural and social influences which are often overlooked by commentators.

This diversity and Southeast Asia's strategic geographical position has made the region a critical trading hub for centuries, starting with the spice trade with Indians, Persians and Arabs in Southeast Asian islands. In more recent times, countries in the region have realized the increased need to adopt a more united approach on the world stage. This gave rise in 1967 to the formation of the Association of Southeast Asian Nations (ASEAN) by five founding member states—Indonesia, Malaysia, the Philippines, Singapore and Thailand. Since then, ASEAN has extended to 10 member countries and deepened regional collaboration in economic growth, social progress and cultural development.

Vietnam acceded to ASEAN in 1995, ten years after the start of economic reforms. Joining ASEAN demonstrated Vietnam's commitment to economic cooperation in the region and to the opening of the economy and to trade liberalization. ASEAN member countries' share in Vietnamese trade amounted already to 28% of imports and of 18% of exports in the year of accession, far exceeding that of any other countries or regions.

6.2 From a Low to a Middle-Income Country

Accession to ASEAN facilitated further economic integration with the world economy through a number of complementary trade agreements, increasing trade levels and economic growth. As a result, Vietnam transitioned from one of the

[1]While Southeast Asia is mostly used to denominate the geographic area, ASEAN refers to intergovernmental agreements of the Southeast Asian states (currently excluding East Timor).

Table 6.1 Nominal GDP and Population Estimates in 2019 for Member Countries of ASEAN. *Source* World Economic Outlook Database (2019)

Country	Nominal GDP per capita	Population (millions)
Singapore	65,627	5.7
Brunei	30,290	0.4
Malaysia	11,385	32.8
Thailand	7,607	67.9
ASEAN	4,747	654.4
Indonesia	4,123	267.0
Philippines	3,280	108.7
Laos	2,931	6.9
Vietnam	2,725	95.5
Cambodia	1,635	16.5
Myanmar	1,238	53.0

world's poorest nations to a middle-income country in 2010.[2] However, the passage to becoming a prosperous and modern economy has only just begun.

With an estimated GDP per capita of US$2,551 in 2019, Vietnam occupies the 136th rank out of 192 countries according to IMF's World economic outlook data. The average GDP per capita in the ASEAN region is around US$4,747 as shown below, placing Vietnam among the three poorest nations in ASEAN, above only Cambodia and Myanmar. In terms of population, Indonesia is the largest of the ASEAN countries (with around 40% of a total 654 million inhabitants), followed by the Philippines and Vietnam with each around 100 million inhabitants (Table 6.1).

In short, Vietnam is a populous but relatively poor country with tremendous potential for socio-economic growth. It can play an important role in the regional transformation towards higher levels of industrialization but there remain important challenges ahead.

The Fig. 6.1 illustrates the trajectory of Vietnam's economic development compared to China, Thailand and South Korea, which are three countries which have experienced similar economic reform moments in their history. All these countries have achieved higher GDP per capita levels 32 years after the reforms have started.[3] It took China 23 years to achieve the current levels of GDP per capita, Thailand 16 years and South Korea started reforming its economy at approximately the same GDP levels as Vietnam in 2018. In this light, an acceleration of the current reforms in Vietnam seems critical to maintain the momentum the country has garnered over the past two decades. To achieve high-income status with US$25,000 GDP per capita,

---

[2]As of 1 July 2018, low-income economies are defined by the World Bank as those with a GNI per capita of $995 or less in 2017; lower middle-income economies are those with a GNI per capita between $996 and $3,895.

[3]The year 1986 is set as the start of reforms for Vietnam ("*Đổi Mới*"), 1978 for China ("Open Door Policy"), and 1972 for both South Korea (continuation of the "Outward Looking Economic Strategy") and Thailand (reforms by the Thanarat regime of infrastructure development and privatization of SOEs).

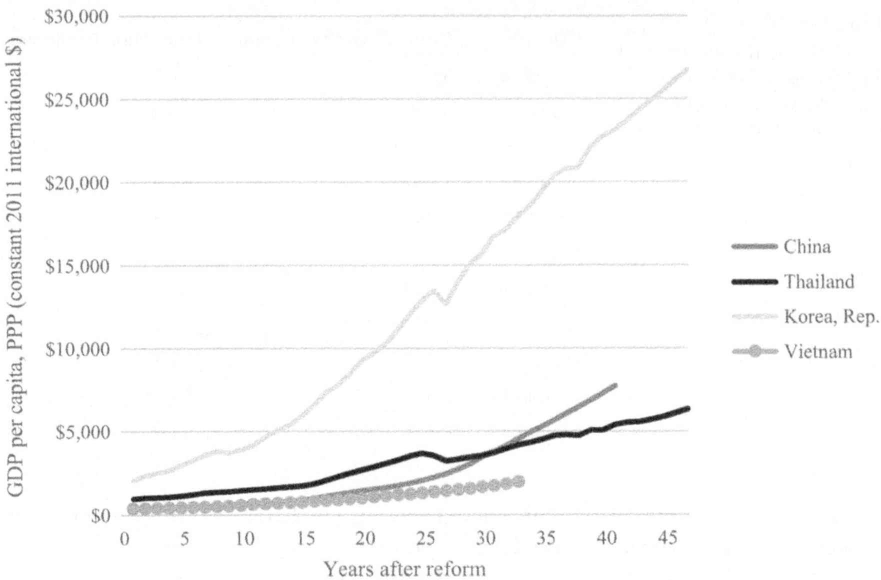

Fig. 6.1 Vietnam's Transition to a Modern Economy Is Not Yet Done. *Source* Adapted from Eckardt and Ngoan (2019) and World Development Indicators, 2019 (0 = year of the start of reforms)

Vietnam needs to sustain a growth rate of around 7.7% per annum for the next 30 years. This is of course ambitious and perhaps overly so and continued reforms are key to achieving high-income status.

As it transpires, the factors that have propelled the economy in the past are diminishing. Returns from economic reforms will be smaller. Productivity may persist at low levels, while a rapidly aging population and fast-growing labour costs may erode Vietnam's comparative advantage as a central hub in certain segments of global value chains.

6.3 Socio-Economic Development Objectives

The government of Vietnam has set several socio-economic targets for the medium term. The National Assembly (2016) created a Resolution (No. 142/2016/QH13 from April 12, 2016) with three broad objectives for the period 2016–2020. In the economic realm, these objectives were maintenance of macroeconomic stability, achievement of economic growth, enhancement of efficiency and competitiveness and acceleration of economic restructuring. In the socio-political sphere, the objectives specified the practice of democracy, social progress and justice, national independence

Table 6.2 Key Socio-Economic Development Targets of the Development Plan 2016–2020. *Source* National Assembly (2016)

1. **Economic targets**
Gross domestic product (GDP) will be around 6.5%–7% on average in five years
GDP per capita will be approximately US$3,200–3,500 by 2020
Industry and services sectors will account for 85% of GDP by 2020
Total social investment will account for approximately 32–34% of GDP on average in five years
State budget deficit will be below 4% of GDP by 2020
Total factor productivity (TFP) will contribute 30–35% to economic growth
Social labour productivity will increase by about 5%/year
Energy consumption based on GDP will reduce by 1%-1.5%/year
Rate of urbanization will reach 38–40% by 2020
2. **Social targets**
Rate of agricultural labour among the total workforce will be around 40% by 2020
Rate of trained workers will reach approximately 65–70% by 2020, of which the rate of workers having diplomas and certificates will reach 25%
Urban unemployment rate will be below 4% by 2020
By 2020, there will be 9–10 doctors and more than 26.5 patient beds per one thousand people
Health insurance coverage will be over 80% of the population by 2020
Poverty rate will reduce by about 1.0–1.5%/year
3. **Environmental targets**
Percentage of population using clean water will be 95% in urban areas and 90% in countryside by 2020
Rate of hazardous waste processed will be 85% by 2020
Rate of medical waste processed will be 95–100% by 2020
Forest cover will reach about 42% by 2020

and sovereignty, peace and stability and to strive to become a "modern-oriented industrialized country."

The Table 6.2 contains a list of the broader policy objectives translated into quantifiable targets for the year 2020. Overall, the government aims to achieve rapid, environmentally sustainable and socially equitable economic growth.

Vietnam has already met or exceeded most of the key socio-economic goals at the end of 2018. However, emerging tensions in global trade in 2019 and the possibility of a global economic downturn accompanying the ongoing coronavirus pandemic make these goals appear ambitious in the next coming years.

The Socio-Economic Development Targets are aligned with Vietnam's past sustained economic growth, its commitment to the numerous free trade agreements it has entered and to the United Nations Sustainable Development Goals.

While the Socio-Economic Development Plan explicitly contains environmental targets, it does not reflect the rapidly rising pollution resulting from increased manufacturing activity and the commitments with the Paris Climate Agreement, which it ratified in 2016. Vietnam agreed to an 8% reduction in annual emissions with domestic means by 2030 when compared to the "business as usual" scenario (Neefjes 2018). The commitment to the Paris Climate Agreement is motivated by the increased frequency and severity of natural disasters that Vietnam has experienced in the last decade. As these natural disasters disproportionally affect poor and rural communities, any measures to decrease the impact of climate change provide important social, environmental and health benefits (Neefjes 2018).

There are barriers to overcome to achieve the various environmental commitments. One such barrier is a lack of a clear definition of a green growth strategy and how to tackle the commitments made. Another barrier is that policy-makers view industrial development and environmental protection as competing priorities. Recent policy decisions demonstrate a preference for economic growth and industrial development to attract more foreign investment. Clearly, policy-makers still need a strategy and framework to sustain economic growth while meeting the environmental targets.

6.4 Economic Growth, Productivity and Competitiveness

Since 2010, Vietnam's GDP growth has exceeded 5% every year and, in 2018, growth peaked at 7.0% (although the coronavirus pandemic will halt that progress). With such rapid economic expansion, the country grew from one of the poorest countries in the world to a comfortably middle-income one. Whereas its GDP per capita was barely $230 in 1985, by 2018, corrected for purchasing power, it stood at over $6,000.

Despite the sustained growth in GDP, labour productivity lags significantly behind countries in the region, as shown below. With a labour force of 54 million employed persons and 1.1 million unemployed persons, Vietnam's labour productivity currently stands behind almost all countries in Southeast Asia, including Lao PDR (ILOSTAT 2019).

In 2016, the average productivity of a Vietnamese employee reached $11,100, equalling 7% of that of Singapore, 17% of Malaysia and 36% of Thailand. This low labour productivity is attributed in part to the relatively low starting point as an agricultural-dominated economy and in part to an inefficient economic structure where SOEs had a dominant position in the economy (Fig. 6.2).

Agriculture, forestry and fisheries makes up 16.3% of the Vietnamese economy, while the proportion in Thailand is 8%, 10% in the Philippines and 14% in Indonesia. In Singapore, at the other end of the spectrum, industry, construction and services sectors make up nearly 100%.

With a declining share of agriculture in the national GDP and simultaneous upskilling of the labour force, the Vietnamese government expects that labour productivity will rise rapidly over the next few years. Without doubt, labour-intensive sectors continue to be the growth drivers for Vietnam's economic development. As the world moves towards Industry 4.0 with higher degrees of automation and concurrent demand for semi-skilled and skilled labour, the government should introduce significant reforms across all the main sectors of the economy to remain competitive.

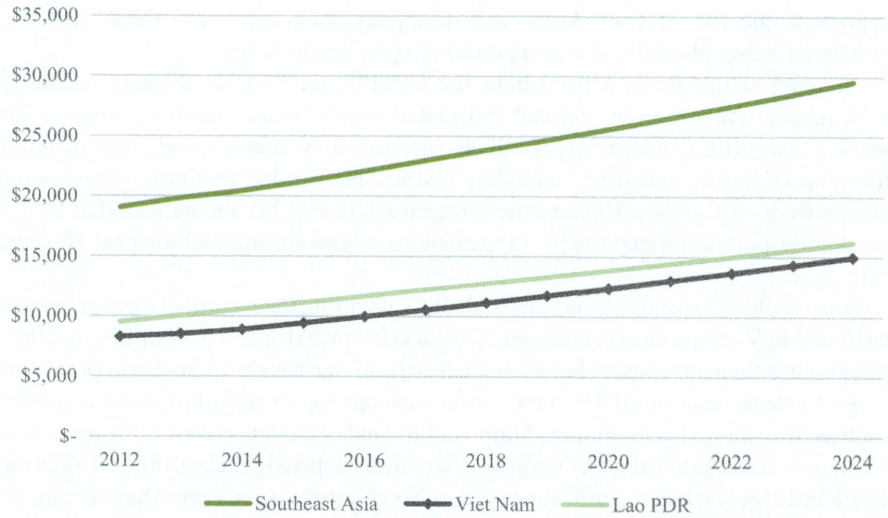

Fig. 6.2 Output per Worker. *Source* ILO Modelled Estimates (ILOSTAT 2019) (GDP constant 2011 international $ in PPP)

6.5 Trade as a Major Contributor to Economic Growth

Over the past 30 years, Vietnam has pursued an ambitious policy of trade liberalisation, fuelling the remarkable growth and making it a posterchild of the benefits of an open economy. To date, it has signed 26 trade agreements with different partners, promoting the country as one of the main manufacturing hubs in the world. In 1995, Vietnam joined the ASEAN community and consequently became party to several FTAs that the regional trade bloc had signed. In 2000, it signed an FTA with the United States, to be followed by admission to the World Trade Organisation in 2007. Since then, the country has further integrated itself into the world economy with bilateral agreements with regional neighbours such as China, India, Japan and South Korea, as recently occurred with the signing of the Regional Comprehensive Economic Partnership (RCEP. Vietnam was also the main driver behind the 11-country Comprehensive and Progressive Agreement for Trans-Pacific Partnership (CPTPP) which came into force in December, 2018.

In 2019, Vietnam entered two agreements between the EU and Vietnam known as the EVFTA: a free trade agreement and an investment protection agreement. Vietnam is the fourth country in Asia which has signed such an agreement with the EU, after high-income countries Japan, South Korea and Singapore. The EVFTA is the most ambitious free trade deal ever concluded between the European countries and a developing country. The agreement will result in the almost complete elimination of customs duties between the two partners. Duties on EU exports to Vietnam will decrease by 65% as soon as the FTA enters into force, while the remainder will be phased out gradually over a period of up to ten years. Similarly, for Vietnamese exports to the EU 71% of duties will disappear upon entry into force, with the remainder being phased out over a period of up to seven years.

Vietnam stands to gain from both the CPTPP and EVFTA through increased FDI, further integration in regional and global supply chains and a growing export market share. Both agreements are likely to augment Vietnam's trade opportunities for many of its key industries, including textiles, leather and footwear, e-commerce and services. By some estimates, these recent FTAs will lift Vietnam's GDP by 1.3 percentage points and exports by 4.0 percentage points throughout the next 15 years (Fig. 6.3).

As a result of Vietnam's policy of trade liberalization, the weighted average import tariff rate in Vietnam stood at around 2.7% of GDP in 2018, down from 19% in 2000. It is perhaps then no wonder that Vietnam has the highest trade intensity (imports plus exports as a percent of GDP) in the world—except for a handful of small countries such as Singapore, Luxembourg, Malta and Ireland. The figure above illustrates that Vietnam's trade intensity has steadily risen from approximately 100% of GDP to 188% in 2018. During the same time span, other countries in the region have declining (e.g. Indonesia and Malaysia) or relatively stable (e.g. Cambodia and Thailand) trade indicators. Vietnam's trade intensity largely exceeded the global (58%) and regional (42%) averages as well as that of low-income countries (56%) in 2018.

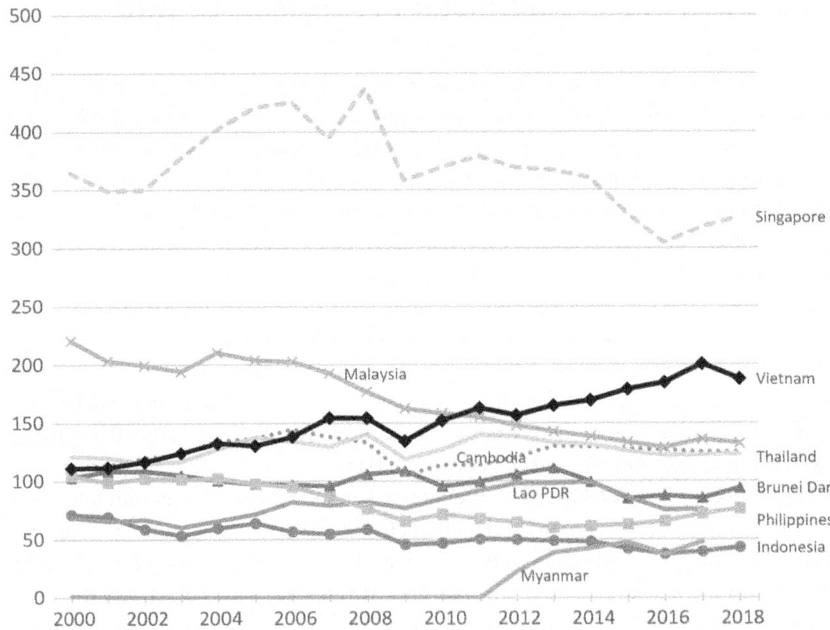

Fig. 6.3 Trade as a Percentage of GDP for Selected Southeast Asian Countries. *Source* Adapted from World Bank (2019)

International trade has been a centrepiece of Vietnam's economic policies in the recent past and without doubt the resulting economic integration came with positive spill overs, such as rising incomes and increased competitiveness. However, it remains unlikely that the high level of trade will provide enough momentum to sustain growth rates in the decades to come.

6.6 A Rapidly Aging Society Engenders Cultural, Social and Economic Reforms

Over the past thousand years, Vietnam has borrowed many ideals and norms from its Chinese neighbour. Among many others, the implementation of the one-or-two child policy to lower fertility rates has influenced its social development until today.

In 1963, the socialist government of North Vietnam planned to set a policy to reduce the annual population growth rate from 3.5% to 2% (Vu 1992). This policy encouraged couples to limit their family sizes to two or three children, with five to six years in between each child. However, the policy's effectiveness was constrained by the scarcity of resources due to the protracted war period (1955–1975). Moreover, the number of fatalities during wartime called for population growth. Increasing population growth was an attempt to make up for the lives lost to war while gaining the ability to send more people to the battlefield.

After the American war ended in 1975, Vietnam stepped into an era of industrialization and modernization. Economic disincentives mitigated excessive childbearing and made people cognizant of family size and population growth. If fertility rates kept increasing even after Vietnam became independent, the country's population would continue to accelerate, with negative economic consequences. As a result, the government formulated an anti-natalist population policy, as described above and this was formally adopted in 1988. Unlike its coercive one-child counterpart in China, this initiative was less draconian and applied chiefly to government cadres. Further, 13% of Vietnam's ethnic minority groups could have up to three children. Overall, the role of fertility policies and economic reforms effectively lowered the fertility rate in Vietnam.

Why did Vietnam choose to implement the one-or-two child policy? First, the lack of resources and institutional rigor to coerce a one-child initiative made this alternative impractical (Feeney and Wang 1993). Second, continuing the encouragement of a two-or-three child policy would lead to an uncontrollable increase in population growth. Consequently, the onset of the one-or-two child policy legitimized a family to have one child and a second if desired.

Vietnam's family planning policy has played a vital role in fertility decline since the 1970s. Before, a large, crowded family meant many children could take care of their parents. However, this was followed by a downward trajectory of fertility and family size. As a result, the government formed nursing homes with caregivers to

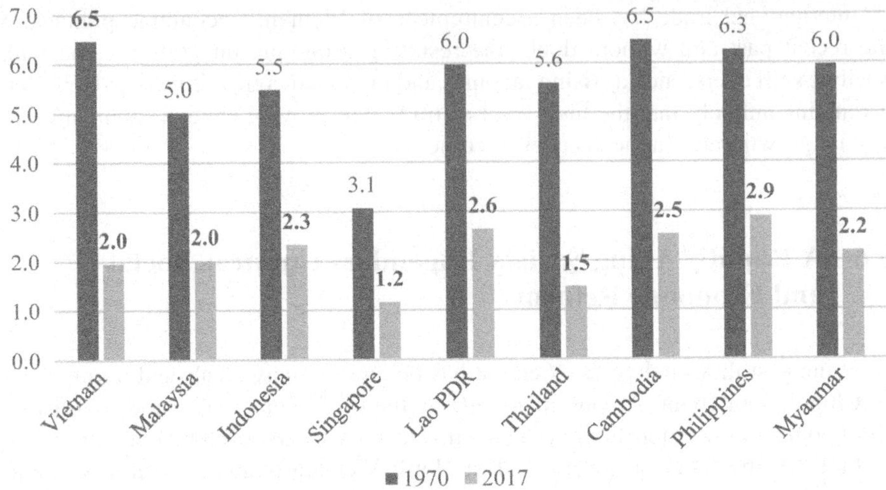

Fig. 6.4 Total Fertility Rates (Births per Woman) in 1970 and 2017. *Source* Adapted from World Development Indicators (2019)

take care of the elderly. The older Vietnamese generation now has alternative options for retirement, rather than solely relying on their children as they did in the past.

However, with a largely rural population, the political disincentives for large families took effect only with concurrent urbanization. The figure below illustrates the decline in fertility rates across South-East Asia. These dropped significantly, from an average of about 5.6 births per woman in 1970 to 2.1 in 2017. This represents a 70% decline versus 62% for the region during the period 1970–2017. The public policy measures compounded by socio-econometric changes are perhaps the reasons for the lowest fertility rates in Southeast Asia (except Singapore) in 2017. As a result, Vietnam is the fastest-aging society not only in Southeast Asia but in the world (Fig. 6.4).

This demographic shift is important for many reasons. First, it signifies the end of an intergenerational contract and the typical family structure in Vietnam, in which two or more generations support each other and the beginning of a society based on nuclear family structures. The government took note of this. Several community-based eldercare models are being implemented across the country. At the same time. the public healthcare system has not yet caught up with the drastic demographic change. For example, only a fraction of city and province level hospitals offer gerontological services. While public policy initiatives may avert the worst for the elderly, it is likely that market-based mechanisms will fill some of the gaps in supply of services to the elderly.

Second, the fast-aging population goes along with the need to review policies related to the elderly, including the Law on Elderly, the Social Insurance Law and the Population Ordinance. Encouraging or forcing the younger generation to save for their own retirement and eldercare is an important piece of the political toolbox currently being debated.

Addressing the consequences of Vietnam's aging population is both a public policy challenge and a cultural challenge. Increasing the retirement age from currently 60 years for men and 55 for women to 62 and 60 respectively is proposed by the Ministry of Labour, Invalids, and Social Affairs. This, together with policy measures to increase participation of women and elderly in the workforce and incentives to increase birth rates are first steps in the right direction to address the fundamental demographic shift happening in contemporary Vietnam.

6.7 Corruption as a Damper to Economic Growth and Equitable Distribution of Wealth

The prevalence of corruption remains high in Vietnam and threatens its future economic growth. Corruption is commonly defined as the abuse of public power for private gain and includes petty and grand corruption (Kaufmann et al. 2011). An enduring perception of corruption in Vietnam has been captured by the Corruption Perception Index (CPI) published by Transparency International since 1997. The Vietnam Provincial Governance and Public Administration Performance Index (PAPI) 2018 shows a slight improvement in the perceived control of corruption over the last three years (CECODES et al. 2019).

The CPI ranked Vietnam at 117th among 180 countries in 2018 (CPI 2018). Vietnam's rank has not shown significant improvement since the first CPI survey in 2012 and is still at the 35th percentile. In the same report, 65% of survey participants in Vietnam had reportedly paid a bribe when accessing public services, which is the second highest rate in Asia Pacific, after India. The government's efforts to fight corruption is still regarded as ineffective, due to deep interference of corrupt officials in approving the anti-corruption law (ACL) (Transparency International and Towards Transparency 2017) (Fig. 6.5).

The strong relationship between GDP per capita and perceived levels of corruption has been shown in numerous academic studies (see, e.g., Mauro 1995) and is also obvious in the Southeast Asian context. Singapore is perceived as being the least corrupt country, scoring in the 98th percentile. At the other end of the spectrum, Cambodia is the most corrupt country, ranking in the 11th percentile.

It is, therefore, notable that Vietnam has not improved its control of corruption over a decade which has experienced strong economic growth. However, a closer look reveals that none of the Southeast Asian countries have significantly improved their CPI scores over the period 2012 to 2018 except Myanmar.[4] The inertia of

[4]Myanmar has experienced a fundamental reform of its political structure between 2011 and 2015 towards a liberal democracy and a "mixed" economy, which explains a doubling of its CPI score between 2012 and 2018.

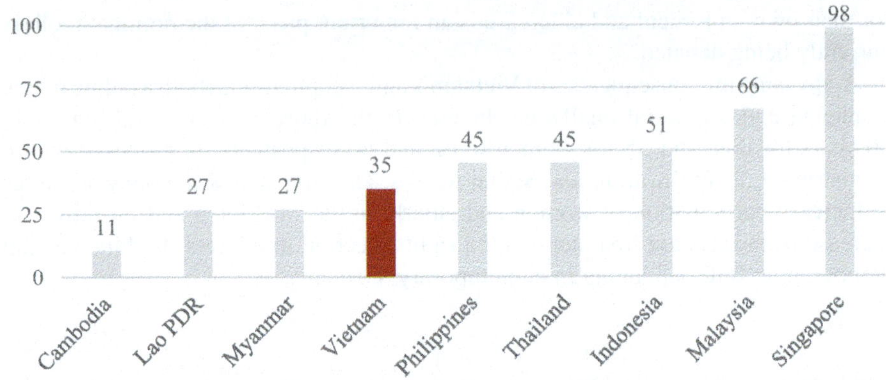

Fig. 6.5 Percentile Rank in CPI in 2018 for ASEAN. *Source* Adapted from Corruption Perception Index (2018) (excluding Brunei)

corruption scores in the region and in Vietnam is due to deep-rooted cultural and systemic idiosyncrasies.

In Vietnam, the low pay for government officials and a lack of monitoring create conflicts of interests in the public sector, which contributes to the widespread corruption (Gregory 2016). Without strict monitoring and inspection, public officials supplement their income with bribes in their transactions with citizens (MacLean 2012). 65% of Vietnamese citizens are reported to have paid bribes to access six key public services (police, public healthcare, public education, court, utilities, issuance of ID card and other permits (Transparency International 2017)), with the highest bribery rates surveyed for police, public school and healthcare (*ibid.*). Vietnam's bribery rate is the highest among ASEAN countries and the second highest in Asia Pacific, after India at 68%. Firms operating in Vietnam also must often deal with graft in their transactions with state authorities. Bureaucratic procedures force businesses to give informal payments to grease the wheel and speed up the process (Maruichi and Abe 2019). Meanwhile, the practice of gift-giving to public authorities or supervisors in the company is considered a norm and small graft payments thus disguise petty corruption as an expected way to facilitate business process or to achieve personal interests (Nguyen et al. 2016). Corruption at a larger scale or grand corruption, in which elite actors arrange deals and abuse state policies to extract the state budget for personal gains, is also rife in the government (Tran 2019). The high rate of economic growth after the time of the *Đổi Mới* programme has allowed corruption to flourish, as high-ranking government officials can now commodify their authority over the equitization of state assets (Gregory 2016).

The trajectory of corruption in Vietnam is similar to the "double paradox" observed in China, when the transfer of ownership from the public to the private sectors created unprecedented economic growth but not without creating entrenched corruption among the most high-ranking party officials (Wedeman 2012; Gregory 2016). Corruption, along with bureaucracy, negatively affects the business environment in Vietnam (Maruichi and Abe 2019). About 55% of businesses surveyed in the

Vietnam Provincial Competitiveness Index 2018 reportedly paid 'informal charges' to authorities (Malesky et al. 2019). The ease of starting and doing business in Vietnam remains low at 104th and 69th out of 190 countries, respectively (World Bank 2019). Nguyen et al. (2016) reported a troubling finding that Vietnamese firms were expected to pay bribes to overcome delays caused by the inefficient public sector. In other developing countries such as China, bribery has been found to undermine growth of firms, particularly small- and medium-sized firms (Zhou and Peng 2011). In the Indonesian manufacturing industry, corruption appeared to facilitate the productivity of bribe-giving plants (usually by large firms) at the expense of the small firms who could not offer comparable bribes and of the industry at the aggregate level (Vial and Hanoteau 2010).

According to Ha (2013), persistent corruption taints the public perception of the CPV and challenges its legitimacy. The former General Secretary Nong Duc Manh acknowledged that corruption was "… one of the major risks that threaten the survival of our regime" in his speech at the 10th Party Congress in 2006. The fear of political instability prompted action from the government to strengthen governance and curb corruption. Prior to the 10th Party Congress, an anti-corruption law (ACL) was passed in 2005, establishing anti-corruption measures such as assets declaration, job rotation and regulations of gift-giving practice.

Despite these efforts from the government, corruption remained a pressing issue after a decade of implementation of the ACL, with the government being cognizant of the impasse:

> Corruption remains complex, happens at many levels and sectors, and has not been driven back. In general, anti-corruption efforts have not achieved the set objectives and contain many weaknesses.
>
> - Government report, No. 330/BC-CP, dated 22 September 2016, page 15.

In 2018, the government strengthened the ACL, extending the law to include private sector transactions and to give more power to inspecting agencies, in particular the Government Inspectorate of Vietnam. The 2018 ACL attempts to control conflicts of interest and cronyism among those in management positions and former officials.

While the 2018 ACL enhanced the legal framework, it is uncertain whether the law will prove more effective in its implementation. A lack of transparency, undue political influence over inspecting agencies and a failure to protect whistle-blowers of corrupt practices all limit the effectiveness of Vietnam's anti-corruption strategy (IMF 2019). Furthermore, limited media freedom and power collusion under a one-party government dampens the effort to control corruption. Thayer (2006) wrote in the *Wall Street Journal*: "While continuing corruption may be a threat to the party's grip on power, tackling it properly would pose an even bigger threat."

6.8 Summary

This chapter has reviewed facets of the recent socio-economic history of Vietnam in an international context. The country has shown a remarkable transition from a low- to middle-income country. Vietnam has set ambitious economic and social development objectives, to continue these achievements. Trade has been a key ingredient in attaining government targets in past. the future trajectory remains uncertain. Important challenges to continue this growth arise from persistent low labour productivity, an aging society and endemic corruption.

Acknowledgements The authors would like to thank Nguyen Hanh Nga for her capable research assistance.

References

CECODES, VFF-CRT, RTA & UNDP (2019) The 2018 Vietnam Governance and Public Administration Performance Index (PAPI): Measuring Citizens' Experiences. A Joint Policy Research Paper by Centre for Community Support and Development Studies (CECODES), Centre for Research and Training of the Vietnam, Fatherland Front (VFF-CRT), Real-Time Analytics, and United Nations Development Programme (UNDP). http://papi.org.vn/wp-content/uploads/2019/03/2018PAPIREPORT_VIE_FINAL.pdf. Accessed 20 September 2019

Corruption Perception Index (CPI) database (2018) Transparency Int. https://www.transparency.org/cpi2018. Accessed 16 September 2019

Eckardt S, Ngoan V (2019, May 16) How can Vietnam avoid the middle-income trap? The Brookings Institution. https://www.brookings.edu/blog/future-development/2019/05/16/how-can-vietnam-avoid-the-middle-income-trap. Accessed 19 September 2019

Feeney G, Feng W (1993) Parity progression and birth intervals in china: the influence of policy in hastening fertility decline. Population Develop Rev 1:60–101

Gregory R (2016) Combating corruption in Vietnam: a commentary. Asian Educ Develop Studies 5(2):227–243. https://doi.org/10.1108/AEDS-01-2016-0010

Ha HH (2013) Trends in Southeast Asia: More change awaits Vietnam's political economy. ISEAS Publishing, Singapore

ILOSTAT database (2019) Department of Statistics, International Labour Organization. https://ilostat.ilo.org. Accessed 10 September 2019

International Monetary Fund (2019, July 16) Five Charts Explain Vietnam's Economic Outlook. Int Monetary Fund. https://www.imf.org/en/News/Articles/2019/07/11/na071619-five-charts-explain-vietnams-economic-outlook. Accessed 1 October 2019

Kaufmann D, Kraay A, Mastruzzi M (2011) The worldwide governance indicators: methodology and analytical issues. Hague J Rule Law 3(2):220–246. https://doi.org/10.1017/S1876404511200046

MacLean K (2012) Enacting anticorruption: the reconfiguration of audit regimes in contemporary Vietnam. Positions: Asia Critique 20(2):595–625

Malesky E, Phan TN, Pham NT (2019) The Vietnam provincial competitiveness index: measuring economic governance for private sector development, final report. Hanoi, Vietnam: Vietnam Chamber of Commerce and Industry and United States Agency for International Development

Maruichi D, Abe M (2019) Corruption and the business environment in Vietnam: implications from an empirical study. Asia Pacific Policy Studies 6(2):222–245. https://doi.org/10.1002/app5.275

Mauro P (1995) Corruption and growth. Q J Econ 110(3):681–712. https://doi.org/10.2307/2946696
National Assembly (2016) Resolution on Five-year Socio-economic Development Plan From 2016–2020—The National Assembly of The Socialist Republic of Vietnam. Policy Document. Vietnam Government Portal. http://www.chinhphu.vn/portal/page/portal/English/strategies/strategiesdetails?categoryId=30&articleId=10057712. Accessed 19 August 2019
Neefjes K (2018) Long-term greenhouse gas emission mitigation opportunities and drivers in Vietnam: meeting paris agreement targets and accelerating progress towards the SDGs. policy paper. UNDP Vietnam. https://www.vn.undp.org/content/vietnam/en/home/library/environment_climate/long-term-greenhouse-gas-emission-mitigation-opportunities-and-d.html
Nguyen N, Doan Q, Nguyen N, Tran N (2016) The impact of petty corruption on firm innovation in Vietnam. Crime Law Soc Change 65(4–5):377–394
Thayer CA (2006, April 27) Vice in Vietnam. The Wall Street Journal. https://www.wsj.com/articles/SB114608623105236787. Accessed 20 September 2019
Tran LT (2019, March 4) Vietnam and the fight against corruption. Nikkei Asian Rev. https://asia.nikkei.com/Opinion/Vietnam-and-the-fight-against-corruption. Accessed 20 September 2019
Transparency International & Towards Transparency (2017) 2017 Global Corruption Barometer: Vietnam—Views and experiences from Vietnamese citizens. Report. Hong Duc Publishing House. https://towardstransparency.vn/wp-content/uploads/2019/02/Towards-Transparency-Newsletter-Dec-2017.pdf
Vial V, Hanoteau J (2010) Corruption, manufacturing plant growth and the Asian paradox: Micro-level evidence from Indonesia. World Dev 38(5):693–705
Vu QN (1992) Population policies and development in Vietnam. In: Jamieson N, Nguyen MH, Rambo AT (eds) The Challenges of Vietnam's Reconstruction. Indochina Institute of George Mason University, Fairfax, VA, USA, pp 40–54
Wedeman A (2012) Double paradox: rapid growth and rising corruption in China. Cornell University Press, Ithaca, NY
World Bank (2019) Doing Business 2019: training for reform. Economy profile for Vietnam (16th ed.). The World Bank Group. https://doi.org/10.1596/978-1-4648-1326-9
World Development Indicators database (2019) World Bank. https://databank.worldbank.org/source/world-development-indicators. Accessed 19 August 2019
World economic outlook database (2019) International Monetary Fund. https://www.imf.org/external/pubs/ft/weo/2019/01/weodata/index.aspx. Accessed 19 August 2019
Worldwide Governance Indicators database (2019) World Bank. https://info.worldbank.org/governance/wgi. Accessed 19 August 2019
Zhou JQ, Peng MW (2011) Does bribery help or hurt firm growth around the world? Asia Pacific J Manag 29(4):907–921

Chapter 7
Environmental Impact

7.1 Introduction

With a total land territory of 331,210 km^2, Vietnam is the world's 67th largest country, although its population of 97 million makes it the world's 15th most populous. The population is unevenly distributed across the country, with the Red (*Hồng*) and Mekong delta regions the most densely occupied and with good representation along the 3,444 km of coastline (excluding islands) (CIA 2019). Nearly 35% of the total land has been given to agriculture, with 45% under forest land cover and 20% under other forms of land cover. Its location in the sub-tropical climate zone and extensive coastline contributes to Vietnam's vulnerability to seasonal cyclones and related phenomena.

In common with most countries, Vietnam suffers from the stressful impacts on the natural environment of industrialisation and economic transformation, including pollution, urbanization, threat to wildlife and contamination of groundwater. These impacts are potentially worse than in other countries which have undergone rapid economic change because of the very late stage at which it has been taking place. In contrast with, for example, South Korea or Malaysia, Vietnam is undergoing the progress when it has become undeniable that the effects of global climate change pose an existential threat to humanity, after the 2008 financial crisis when expansionary economic conditions no longer apply and when China has already emerged as a global superpower with its own agenda for international relations and for patterns of trade and investment. Although technological improvements have mitigated some negative impacts on the environment and may do more in the future, it is also true that the country and its leadership are constrained by external factors which were not prevalent to the same extent in the past. Vietnam suffers from one additional environmental impact which separates it from most other countries and that is the ongoing effects of the long wars which the country endured. This chapter will begin with a consideration of this impact from the past on the present and then move on to analyse pollution and related events, rapid urbanization, water management and the

J. Walsh et al., *The Political Economy of Vietnam's Industrial Transformation*,
SpringerBriefs in Political Science,
https://doi.org/10.1007/978-981-16-0151-4_7

likely impacts of global climate change, particularly with respect to agriculture, The chapter concludes with some of the technologies and concepts which might mitigate these negative impacts in the future.

7.2 The Shadow of the Past

During the Second Indochina War or the American War in Vietnam (1955–75), the American forces responded to the heavily forested land of the battlefields of Vietnam by committing ecocide: aerial bombardment by American air forces using the chemical Agent Orange defoliated approximately five million acres of land (c.2.02 million ha.) so as to expose the movements of troops seeking cover (Zierler 2011:2). This bombardment continues to have negative effects until the present (Do 2009). Numerous examples of elevated risks of disease have been recorded, as well as birth defects (Ngo et al. 2006) such as spina bifida, cerebral palsy, physical and mental retardation and missing or deformed limbs (Satchell 1999). The chemical persisted in the environment, either settling into humid and low-lying areas such as wetlands or lakes and thence accumulating in the tissues of fish and shrimps, whence it entered into the food chain. Ingestion of contaminated items continues into the present (Andrei 2019).

The overall impacts of this ecocide have not been fully measured, owing in part to limitations to technical capacity and because some second or third order effects are difficult to predict let alone quantify. Added to the problems of unexploded ordinance (estimated at over 800,000 tons strewn across the country overall) as well as land mines (MAG n.d.), the legacy of Agent Orange represents a significant environmental problem that has not been properly accounted for and for which reparations are unlikely ever to be made. This is partly a political issue, since it is unlikely that the US and its corporations will acknowledge their actions in any way that might leave them open to any claim for reparations. However, it is also partly a methodological one because of, in the words of Vietnam's leading environmental historian "… how to describe environmental phenomena with multiple and often divergent cascades of causal effects in different social, economic and ecological settings (Biggs 2018)."

As the country moves towards more intensive forms of capitalist production, the environmental history of Vietnam is likely to be buried beneath more recent ecological crises (as shown below) and memories will be effectively suppressed. After all, much of the history of modern Vietnam has been centred on the attempt to create a contemporary state that embraced the aesthetic of the Communism of the Soviet Union while it was "… also shaped by its colonial history, both in architectural survival and in anti-colonial rejection (Therborn 2017:270)." The later that rapid economic transformation takes place, the more is there awareness of the past to be overcome in the struggle to achieve what is new.

7.3 Pollution

Air pollution has emerged as a significant health problem in Vietnam and is thought to result in about 60,000 deaths per year through the heart disease, stroke, pulmonary disease and lung cancer that it has caused (WHO 2018) or to which it contributes. Numerous factors help exacerbate this problem, including industrial effluence and the results of more traditional activities such as straw burning (Viet Nam News 2019), which is a blight across most of Southeast Asia.

The pollution is intensified by the extensive use of coal-fired plants across the north of Vietnam and the concentration of industry around the capital, which has meant that Hanoi has at least briefly achieved the dubious distinction of having become the most polluted city in the world (Samuel 2019). Environmental problems appear to be multiplying, with a major mercury leak casing government officials to tell people not to eat food produced in that area and then a brick factory was accused of dumping an oily sludge that led to a tap water crisis for one million people (Channel News Asia 2019).

These problems indicate that success in attracting investment has outweighed the ability of the government to control negative externalities and the limitations of the SEZ policy that was intended, at least in part, to keep a distance between industrial and residential areas. The reality is clear to people on a daily basis because of the extensive use of motor bikes in urban areas, which both contribute to the problem and expose their users directly to it. Some research (Le and Trinh 2016) indicates that although people would be willing to use public transportation if better services were available, the provision of systems such as the proposed metro rail line in Hanoi has become a regularly delayed process. Pollution is likely to remain a significant problem in the country for the foreseeable future.

7.4 Water Management

Vietnam has abundant natural resources of water, with 3,500 large rivers of 10 km or more in length contributing to a total run-off of 830–840 billion m^3. However, some 60% of this water is derived from beyond the country's borders and this indicates an issue with upstream countries (i.e. China) relating to international riverine agreements and the damming of rivers, especially the Red and Mekong rivers that eventually reach Vietnamese territory.

In addition to the nine river network systems that each have a catchment area of 10,000 km^2 or larger, water resources are bolstered by the groundwater resources of some 63 billion m^3 per year (Bay 2015). This is supplemented by artificial bodies of water such as dams and reservoirs which have been built quite extensively across the country for the purposes of hydroelectricity generation, irrigation for agriculture and flood control (Dao 2010). Although not part of the Khmer Empire of the 8th–14th CE, Vietnamese polities may nevertheless have benefited from the hydraulic engineering that enabled Angkor and related communities to manage variations in the monsoon rainfalls that are recorded in the rings of the country's ancient cypress trees (Mithen 2013). However, not all engineering attempts have been successful: clearance of mangrove systems in order to promote black tiger shrimp aquaculture projects have proved to be less than satisfactory and have led to pollution and degradation of natural water resources (Baird 1999).

Nevertheless, the Vietnamese government is aiming to put 2,900 hydropower and irrigation reservoirs into operation, with 240 of these capable of containing more than 28 billion m^3 (Bay 2015). This is part of the government's overall policy of water management which has the following priorities:

- Protecting domestic water resources from water quality decline;
- Ensuring continued access to upstream trans-boundary water resources on which Vietnam is highly dependent and
- Supplying clean accessible water services of sufficient quantity and quality equitably to meet human needs in Vietnam (National Center for Water Resource Planning and Investigation 2015).

This policy makes it clear that water management has a relation to equity issues within society and this is most clearly seen with respect to gender issues. The issues are codified in the 1998 Law on Water Resources (amended in 2012), which clearly states that water management is to be conducted on the basis of equity for all citizens of the country. However, this aspiration is somewhat undermined by the practical issues surrounding access to water resources. Across the country, 65% of households lack a water source on the premises and it routinely falls upon girls to collect clean water from whatever source is available. Similarly, most agricultural and aquacultural activities are conducted by women yet they have many fewer opportunities for ownership of land and the ability to participate in decision-making (Open Development Vietnam 2018).

The principle that is most commonly employed to try to overcome problems with inequitable access and use is Integrated Water Resources Management (IWRM), which is "… a process which promotes the coordinated development and management of water, land and related resources in order to maximise economic and social welfare in an equitable manner without compromising the sustainability of vital ecosystems and the environment (Global Water Partnership 2011)." This approach clearly resonates with Sustainable Development Goal No. 6, which relates to clean water and sanitation. Government indicators suggest substantial progress towards achieving this goal, despite acknowledging the continuing lack of a comprehensive plan for water management and a lack of coordination between relevant stakeholders. For example, the proportion of urban households supplied with tap water has increased to 84.5%, the water loss amount has decreased to 23% and water supply capacity in urban areas has significantly improved. Improvements in rural areas have also taken place (Department for Science, Education, Natural Resources and Environment 2018).

Nevertheless, the problems remain formidable. Rapid urbanization, particularly in Hanoi and Ho Chi Minh City, is placing considerable strain on existing and planned systems, the use of SEZs throughout the country as a means of promoting rapid economic development in various regions brings new strains on existing supplies and the inability to deal with household waste apart from dumping it in rivers is causing significant health and hygiene problems further downstream. In Ho Chi Minh City, for example, rapid urbanization is leading to excessive withdrawal of groundwater resources and annual drawdown has reached 2–3 m (Vo 2007). The need to deal with this issue has become urgent when it is realised that the city, like nearly all the world's large ports, is vulnerable to already existing global change: "… the majority of the world's megacities are in coastal lands threatened by sea level rise. Today, more than 50% of the world's population lives within 120 miles of the sea; by 2025, it is estimated that figure will reach 75% (Dawson 2017:5–6)." Recent research has indicated that most of the city will be inundated by 2050 and an additional 20 million people living in the Mekong delta region will also be forced to leave their homes (Lu and Flavelle 2019).

The most common response by governments and international organizations to threats such as this is to promote the concept of resilience, which incorporates, in the words of the US National Academy of Science "… the ability to prepare and plan for, absorb, recover from, and more successfully adapt to adverse events (Dawson 2017:156)." This approach downplays the need for fundamental change to deal with the systems and structures that have led to the crisis and, instead, optimistically consider the ability of the application of science and human ingenuity to solve emergent problems. Consequently, it is not clear that this approach will in itself provide a sustainable solution to the issue.

A similar response has been proposed to deal with the issue of waste disposal and its effects, although attempts have been yet to bear the fruit anticipated. A Japanese project is the most recent to try to clean Hanoi's notorious To Lich River (see below), which has been condemned to a living death of putrid squalor as a result of untold amounts of household and industrial effluence flowing directly into the water. Results to date suggest that a solution would require intervention on a much more massive scale (Urbanist Hanoi 2019). The effluence flows down to the sea, causing problems to nature and humanity all along the way. Additional examples of firms committing acts of pollution intensifies the problem. Concentrating economic development within specific areas of the country has, it has been argued, already led to unsustainable pressure being placed on the environment, including water supply systems (Duong and Thai 2012) and a period of rebalancing is required (Fig. 7.1).

7.5 Urbanization

As part of mainland Southeast Asia, Vietnam (along with Cambodia, Lao PDR, Myanmar and Thailand) has been part of a region characterised by primate cities (McGee 1967), which are cities in which all the principal economic, social, cultural, political and religious features reside and which have, therefore, very little competition from secondary or provincial cities, since these must defer in all cases to the

Fig. 7.1 Plant Islands to Revivify Hanoi's To Lich River. *Source* Author

capital. Cities tend to be created at the principal residence of the hereditary ruler and represent not just the seat of power but also the claim for legitimacy. Consequently, Hanoi was established as the capital of the northern Dai Viet state that was extensively sinicized by colonization, while Saigon (now Ho Chi Minh City) was the capital of the southern state of the Chams prior to unification of the country at the end of the C15th. Each is located advantageously at the centre of fertile agricultural lands, albeit that the topology of the south of the country has been altered by the action of the delta region of the River Mekong. Both cities have remained in continuous occupation, while capitals such as Phnom Penh and Vientiane have spent periods completely abandoned and another, Naypyidaw, has been created from little more than a village. Vietnamese cities have been stable and central to society.

During the war period, people moved towards the cities as refugees and as their livelihoods as agriculturalists has been destroyed during the fighting. Owing to the French occupation, Saigon had taken on the form of a colonial city, which was designed to accept surplus resources extracted from the country and then ship them to the imperial capital. Such a city has a segmented residential scheme in which colonists are physically separated from colonised by the interpolation of the civil service and merchant classes whose loyalty was to the former because that was the source of their income and status. After success in the Vietnamese civil war, the Communist Party of Vietnam anticipated the cities adopting the features of socialist cities, which would result from socialism as a distinctive mode of production and, therefore, "… the modernist high-rises on the urban fringe and large public spaces, and minimal spatial and social inequality (Sheppard 2000)." However, it was difficult for this restructuring to take place given the nature of the already existing cities and because of the lack of resources and technical capacity under the boycott inflicted upon the country. Further, French colonialism had already imparted a bourgeois capitalist feel to the cities, from the cafes lining Saigon's boulevards to the opera house and department stores of Hanoi (Lees 2015:89). Ultimately, the socialist city structure did not arise in Vietnam because, among other reasons, a unitary mode of production cannot meaningfully be identified as a consistent form, that the mode of production is determinant of societal processes and that national units can be considered as autonomous units of analysis (Sheppard 2000).

Since the period of restructuring, urban management has had to take account of the demands from capitalist endeavours for new and different types of labour and the *hộ khẩu* system of household registration has been revised in 2007 and 2014 as a means of regulating labour migrants (Anh 2017). Meanwhile, in 2008, a sudden announcement was made that the official land area of Hanoi would be increased from 920 to 3,345 km^2, with a concomitant increase in the city's population from 3.5 to 6.3 million and bringing a wide swathe of industrial activities under municipal purview (Turner and Schoenberger 2012). This indicates the importance of economic activities in determining urban success and prestige.

As infrastructure linking cities with provincial areas has improved, more people have found it possible to make a living in urban areas as a result of the agricultural links. Giang, a 45-year old fish seller from Nam Dinh is a mobile street vendor in Hanoi, where he sells fish in water-filled plastic bags. His practice is both entrepreneurial and family-based:

> I raise some of the fish myself, the others I purchase. My hometown in Nam Dinh is where my fish 'workshop' is. I only keep a small number of fish here in Hanoi. I pay 1 million a month [$50] a month to rent a 15 square meter house in Gia Lam. I live there alone, without my wife and kids, because most of the space is taken up by my stuff and the fish tanks (Sasges 2013:134).

However, in the new era of capitalist shopkeeping, street vendors are no longer welcome as they represent a movement back from the envisaged modern nature of the city, the threat of poor sanitation and a means of undermining potential inward investment. It is not surprising, therefore, that some vendors will make a claim to being a 'war hero' to maintain their status (Turner and Schoenberger 2012). By contrast, the state is continuing to nominate new areas in which economic activities are to be concentrated and to be associated with local residential areas for the sake of efficiency (The Hanoi Times 2017).

The promotion of efficiency over spontaneity is extended into the countryside as well. As part of its commitment to equality of treatment for all Vietnamese people, the government is building infrastructure that will better enable members of ethnic minority communities, who may reside in comparatively remote areas, to participate in new economic and social opportunities. This includes transportation infrastructure, health services and the control of epidemics, in particular malaria, as well as improvements in the extent of provision of education services and their quality. The electricity network has been extended and land reclamation projects helped to promote sustainable agriculture on a cooperative basis. These activities will enable ethnic minority people to have a better quality of life while working in the new economic developments that have come to their communities, as well as supporting those Viet (ethnic majority) people who have moved there to help establish the economic initiatives (Van et al. 2016:8).

7.6 Climate Change

It has been clear for some years that extensive land cover change in Vietnam through more intensive use of agriculture and the growth of industry has compromised the ability to deal with global climate change. One notable example of this is the degradation of coastal mangrove systems, which are very important in coping with flooding and storms, since they protect dikes used as sea defences (Tri et al. 1998). Local resources, in combination with location-specific knowledge of farmers and agriculturists can be used to mitigate the impact of climate change. Increasing numbers of storms increases local vulnerability and enhances the possibility of food insecurity, which redeployment of existing resources can mitigate (Nguyen et al. 2013).

These are some of the more obvious examples of global climate change as it is being manifested in Vietnam. In 2020 so far, storms including Linfa and Nangka led to hundreds of deaths and nearly one hundred thousand people losing their homes across the central region (Lampard 2020). Typhoon Molave hit next and was even stronger and the hurricane season was not over yet (Staff and Agencies 2020). Of course, it is not possible to identify individual weather events as being caused specifically by global climate change but there is little doubt that the stream of record temperatures, record storms and forest fires being observed around the world is unprecedented in recorded history.

The effects of change may be felt at a variety of different levels, from the large-scale natural disasters down to the everyday climate change experienced by farmers in rural areas. Vietnam has been classified as one of the five countries most vulnerable to climate change and this is very evident in changes in agricultural conditions, with temperature changes and variable rainfall patterns adding risk to all forms of agricultural production (Trinh 2018). The effects are exacerbated by differential spread of insects and diseases, albeit Vietnamese farmers are among those who have responded to the vicissitudes of the natural world with extensive use of chemical insecticides and fertilisers. Wet paddy rice farming makes extensive use of water and the supply of water has become less predictable both because of climate change but also because of the upstream damming of rivers and the poor treatment of river water more generally. One means of attempting to combat climate change is through the development of smart cities, which is described below. However, impacts on rural communities along the country's lengthy coastline seem likely to have to fend for themselves at least to some extent.

7.7 Smart City Development and Resilience

Vietnamese agencies have been talking about various aspects of smart city development (SCD) since 2010 and have begun to issue official plans and policies from 2015. The first smart city will be Ho Chi Minh City, which will achieve that status by 2030 and then Hanoi will be next, followed by Da Nang, Quang Ninh, Binh Duong and others to follow. The main emphasis of SCD in Vietnam is to make cities more competitive according to the global city concept that assumes a "… convergence in economic base, spatial organization and social structure among the world's major cities (Hill and Kim 2000)."

The two leading cities are envisaged to be part of this global network and measures such as joining the Formula 1 Grand Prix circuit are intended to demonstrate that Vietnam's urban areas are becoming increasingly sophisticated, internationalized and open. To this end, master plans have been drawn up which focus on quality of life, economic competitiveness and public order (through, for example, the use of facial recognition software). Increasingly, the language of sustainable development has entered into the SCD discourse, through considerations of smart water and waste management and traffic management systems that will include substantially enhanced public transportation systems (Thuy 2019). However, there has yet to emerge a clear connection between SCD and resilience of climate change adaptation. Although there is evidence of the need for adaptation in both urban and rural Mekong region communities (Pathirana et al. 2018), most practical activities are taking place at the local authority or provincial level (Viet Nam News 2019b), without an integrated approach that sees cities as being part of the same ecology as the rest of the country. As a result, the main effect of SCD to date has been to position foreign capital closer to the heart of national development (Leducq & Scarwell 2018) and deepened the private-public partnership that now steers state-level developmental goals. It remains to be seen whether this approach will be sufficient to deal with the environmental crises that affect and will affect the country.

7.8 Conclusion

The Factory Asia paradigm of intensive, low labour cost manufacturing that Vietnam has adopted as the means of achieving rapid economic development from low to medium income stats inevitably leads to the generation of a certain number of negative externalities and increases in pressure on the management of natural resources. Other countries which went through the same process were able to do so without the same level of scrutiny that is now possible with mobile telephones and internet connectivity, before the acceptance of the UN's Polluter Pays Principle that has elevated public interest in environmental management and, above all, before global climate change had so firmly grasped hold of the weather systems of the world and rendered so many previously profitable economic activities now untenable. There are clearly opportunities and threats in this situation for Vietnam: additional costs will need to be paid but the benefits of sustainable development are more obviously evident and so stakeholders will be more likely to do what is required to bring them into reality.

References

Andrei M (2019, March 1) Agent orange continues to pollute vietnam environment, Study Finds. ZME Science. www.zmescience.com/ecology/agent-orange-contines-to-pollute-vietnam-environment-stdy-finds/. Accessed 25 October 2019

Anh DN (January, 2017) Rural-to-urban migration in vietnam: trend and institutions. Vietnam's Social-Economic Development: A Social Science Review, No. 88, pp 3–19

Baird IG (1999) Fighting for sustainability in the mekong region. Watershed 4(3):54–6

Bay HV (2015) Water Resources Management in Vietnam: Problems and Solutions, Vietnam Law and Legal Forum (March 24th, 2015), available at: vietnamlawmagazine.vn/water-resources-management-in-vietnam-problems-and-solutions-3366.html

Biggs D (2018) Following Dioxin's drift: agent orange stories and the challenge of metabolic history. Int Rev Environ History 4(1):7–31

Boom or bust: Hanoi pollution crises expose growth risks (2019) Channel News Asia. https://www.channelnewsasia.com/news/asia/boom-or-bust-hanoi-pollution-crises-expose-growth-risks-12026562. Accessed 25 October 2019

Central Intelligence Agency (2019, November 16) Vietnam—The World Factbook. Central Intelligence Agency. https://www.cia.gov/library/publications/the-world-factbook/geos/vm.html. Accessed 25 November 2019

Dao N (2010) Dam development in Vietnam: the evolution of dam-induced resettlement policy. Water Alternatives 3(2):324–40. https://data.opendevelopmentmekong.net/dataset/87e6ff7b-c541-49dd-b0e3-f221b0de2c15/resource/844ed46d-5a64-48bb-a56a-7660d48b3a3e/download/Art3-2-19.pdf

Dawson A (2017) Extreme Cities: the perils and promise of urban life in the age of climate change. Verso, London and New York, NY

Department for Science, Education, Natural Resources and Environment, "Viet Nam's Voluntary National Review on the Implementation of the Sustainable Development Goals" (June, 2018) available at: https://sustainabledevelopment.un.org/content/documents/19967VNR_of_Viet_Nam.pdf

Do Q-T (2009) Agent orange and the prevalence of cancer among the vietnamese population 30 Years after the end of the vietnam war. Policy Research Working Papers (World Bank) (September, 2009), available at: https://doi.org/10.1596/1813-9450-5041

Duong PH, Thai TH (2012) Environmentally sustainable development in the Northern focal economic region of Vietnam. paper presented at the International Conference: Sustainable Manufacturing and Environment Management (2012), available at: www.dl.ueb.vnu.edu.vn/handle/1247/4315

Global Water Partnership, "What Is IWRM?" (July 12th, 2011) available at: www.gwp.org/en/GWP_CEE/about/why/what-is-iwrm/

Hà Nội asks for better straw management to reduce air pollution. (2019, October 4) Viet Nam News. http://vietnamnews.vn/environment/536373/ha-noi-asks-for-better-straw-management-to-reduce-air-pollution.html. Accessed 25 November 2019

Hanoi: Six Industrial Clusters to Be Established (2017, December 5) The Hanoi Times. http://hanoitimes.vn/industrial-zone/2017/12/81E0BC34/hanoi-six-industrial-clusters-to-be-established. Accessed 25 October 2019

Hill RC, Kim JW (2000) Global cities and developmental states: New York, Tokyo and Seoul. Urban Studies 37(12):2167–95

Japan to Help Clean Hanoi's Polluted To Lich River (2019, April 23) Urbanist Hanoi. https://urbanisthanoi.com/hanoi-development/14989-japan-to-help-clean-hanoi-s-polluted-to-lich-river. Accessed 25 October 2019

Lampard A (2020) Vietnam floods and landslides displace 90,000 People as new cyclone nears. The Guardian (October 19th, 2020) available at: www.theguardian.com/world/2020/oct/19/vietnam-floods-and-landslides-displace-90000-people-as-new-cyclone-nears

Le TPL, Trinh TA (2016) Encouraging public transport use to reduce traffic congestion and air pollutant: a cast study of Ho Chi Minh City, Vietnam. Procedia Eng 142:236–43, available at: https://www.sciencedirect.com/science/article/pii/S187770581600401X

Leducq D, Scarwell H-J (2018) Smart Cities in Vietnam: between national implementation and metropolitan strengthening of Hanoi. L'Espace Géographique 47(4):305–322

Lees A, City T (2015) A world history. Oxford University Press, Oxford

Lu D, Flavelle C (2019) Rising Seas Will Erase More Cities by 2050, New Research Shows. The New York Times (October 29th, 2019), available at: www.nytimes.com/interactive/2019/10/29/climate/coastal-cities-underwater.html

MAG, "Vietnam" (n.d.) available at: www.maginternational.org/what-we-do/where-we-work/vietnam/

McGee TG (1969) The Southeast Asian City: a social geography of the primate cities of Southeast Asia. G. bell & Sons, London

Mekong Delta Agriculture Adapts to Climate Change (2019b, September 23) Viet Nam News. https://vietnamnews.vn/society/535772/mekong-delta-agriculture-adapts-to-climate-change.html#uEjbJCCV0PrdlFft.97. Accessed 25 October 2019

Mithen, Steven, Thirst: Water and Power in the Ancient World (London: Weidenfeld and Nicolson, 2020)

National Center for Water Resource Planning and Investigation, "To Ensure the Security of Water Resources for Sustainable Development" (2015) available at: https://data.vietnam.opendevelopmentmekong.net/en/dataset/tich-c-c-d-m-b-o-an-ninh-ngu-n-nu-c-cho-phat-tri-n-b-n-v-ng

Ngo AD, Taylor R, Roberts CL, Nguyen TV (2006) Association between agent orange and birth defects: systematic review and meta-analysis. Int J Epidemiol 35(5):1220–30

Nguyen Q, Hoang MH, Öborn I, van Noordwijk M (2013) Multipurpose Agroforestry as a climate change resiliency option for farmers: an example of local adaptation in Vietnam. Climatic Change 117(1–2):241-57

Open Development Vietnam, "Water Resources" (June 28th, 2018) available at: Vietnam.opendevelopmentmekong.net/topics/water/

Pathirana A, Radhakrishnan M, Quan NH, Zevenbergen C (2018) Managing urban water systems with significant adaptation deficits—unified framework for secondary cities: Part I conceptual framework. Climatic Change 149(1):43–56

Samuel P (2019) How air pollution in vietnam affects the business environment. Vietnam Briefing (October 12th, 2019), available at: www.vietnam-briefing.com/air-pollution-vietnam-affects-business-environment.html/

Sasges G (ed) (2013) It's a living: work and life in Vietnam Today. NUS Press, Singapore

Satchell M (1999) Questions in a village. US News World Report 126:62

Sheppard E (2000) Socialist Cities? Urban Geography 21(8):758–763

Staff and Agencies, "Typhoon Molave: Rescuers Scramble to Find Dozens Buried under Landslides in Vietnam," The Guardian (October 29th, 2020), available at: www.theguardian.com/world/2020/oct/29/typhoon-molave-hundreds-search-for-missing-after-landslides-in-vietnam

Therborn G (2017) Cities of power: the urban, the national, the popular, the global. Verso, London and New York, NY

Thuy B (2019) Vietnam Smart City Drive in Full Swing. Vietnam Investment Review (May 16th, 2019), available at: www.vir.com.vn/vietnam-smart-city-drive-in-full-swing-67768.html

Tri NH, Adger WN, Kelly PM (1998) Natural resource management in mitigating climate impacts: the example of mangrove restoration in Vietnam. Global Environmental Change 8(1):49–61

Trinh TA (2018) The Impact of climate change on agriculture: findings from households in Vietnam. Environ Resource Econ 71:897–921
Turner S, Schoenberger L (2012) Street vendor livelihoods and everyday politics in Hanoi, Vietnam: the seeds of a diverse economy? Urban Studies 49(5):1027–1044
Van DN (2016) Chu thai son and luu hung, ethnic minorities in Vietnam. The Gioi Publishers, Hanoi
Vo PL (2007) Urbanization and water management in Ho Chi Minh City, Vietnam: Issues, Challenges and Perspectives. Geo J 70(1):75–89
Water resources management in Vietnam: Problems and solutions (2015, March 24) Vietnam Law & Legal Forum. http://vietnamlawmagazine.vn/water-resources-management-in-vietnam-problems-and-solutions-3366.html. Accessed 25 November 2019
World Health Organization (WHO) More than 60,000 Deaths in Viet Nam Each Year Linked to Air Pollution (May 2nd, 2018) available at: www.who.int/vietnam/news/detail/02-05-2018-more-than-60-000-deaths-in-viey-nam-each-year-linked-to-air-pollution
Zierler D (2011) The invention of ecocide: agent orange, Vietnam, and the scientists who changed the way we think about the environment. University of Georgia Press, Athens, GA

Chapter 8
Conclusion

8.1 Should Strong Government or Market Forces Lead the Next Wave of Development?

Vietnam is at a crossroads. By the end of 2019, some 33 years into the structural reform process of transitioning towards a market-driven economy, policy choices need to be made to maintain the momentum gathered during the past decade. This book took stock of the institutional contingencies, the economic realities, and the socio-cultural constraints of the choice set at hand to sustain development and continue the economic integration in the world economy. Vietnam was late with its transition towards markets, and even later with its industrialization process. In her influential analysis of South Korea's late industrialization, Amsden (1989) highlighted that state dominance in the economy—rather than widely accepted free market principles—were the foundations of development. The prominent role of the state in the development of South Korea is not unique; it is a paradigmatic example of a more general case of late industrialization, observed in countries such as Japan, Taiwan, or Brazil. Amsden (1989) also demonstrated late industrialization being distinct from the dominant type of textbook examples of economic development: Late industrialization is based on learning, or catching up, rather than innovation (e.g., Germany and the USA) or invention (e.g., Britain). This, in essence, is the dilemma that the policy choices need to resolve for Vietnam: will it strive to be another South Korea with a strong state or are its ambitions to become a more "Western" market driven economy?

In order to shed light on this fundamental question, we review several dimensions of the political economy of Vietnam. Chapter 2 has highlighted critical drivers of the more recent economic integration—notably trade. In this chapter, we also show that there are structural conditions which put the future development of Vietnam in peril. Policy makers need to address the multi-layered and long-term effects of an ageing population. Drastic changes in workforce demographics are particularly sensitive

J. Walsh et al., *The Political Economy of Vietnam's Industrial Transformation*,
SpringerBriefs in Political Science,
https://doi.org/10.1007/978-981-16-0151-4_8

in an economy that has touted its young, semi-skilled, and affordable workforce to foreign investors. In addition, low labour productivity and an overall inefficient allocation process across different markets (knowledge and technology, product, credit, and labour markets) arise from weak regulations and a public apparatus that is ineffective. Public institutions an all levels and across services need to be reformed with the goal to increase accountability and transparency. In the foreign relations arena, tensions in the East Sea with Vietnam's largest trading partner China represents a looming threat to further secure Vietnam's role in the global value chain across different industries.

While the economic achievements during the post-*Đổi Mới* period are attributable to the gradual injection of market forces, one may wonder about the role of government authorities and public administration in this process. Chapter 3 focuses squarely on this important question. To accompany the structural economic reforms, the government initiated the public administrative reform in earnest only in 1999, some 13 years after beginning the economic transition. This tardiness may, perhaps, be at the core of the late adoption of market reforms at first. The goals of the Public Administration Reform (PAR) encompassed administrative process simplification, accountability, coordination, transparency, professionalism, and corruption reduction. After an initial ten-year period, the results of the PAR were disappointing, leading to a second ten year of PAR. Progress has been made since. But according to the World Economic Forum (2016) and numerous other commentators, public management including inefficient government bureaucracy, government instability, and poor work ethics in the public administration dampen seriously Vietnam's attractiveness as a place to do business. The public administration is ineffectiveness is grounded in pervasive corruption, a generally unmeritocratic promotion system, and challenges to involving of citizens in public decisions and demanding accountability. In this chapter, we argue that there are several underlying reasons for this. A discrepancy between the power on the one hand and the responsibility on the other of key public servants—all the way to the Prime Minister—with additional interference from the CPV into the government's decision-making leads to unclear allocation of de facto responsibilities. Additionally, the public sector employs more than 10% of the Vietnamese workforce is bloated and staffed with largely inefficient, unmotivated, and unqualified civil servants at the same time. Comparably low salaries in the public sector precludes hiring talented and motivated staff. Finally, the relationship-based system in Vietnam takes often the form of patronage and nepotism, resulting in overall inefficiencies, be it in the private and public sectors. These are structural, historical burdens to be resolved. No wonder it took twenty years to register only timid successes. But if Vietnam wants to choose a future with state-led development, the PAR needs to be accelerated, deepened. An efficient, transparent, and accountable public administration is a *sine qua non* condition for Vietnam to leverage its many other economic, cultural, historic, and social advantages.

In addition to reforming the public sector, privatization is often considered a core element in the transition to a market-driven economy. Here, Vietnam has registered mixed results. In Chap. 4 we expound on the change of ownership—from public to private—and on the ensuing corporate governance frameworks. We show that privatizations have started somewhat late compared to the start of the economic reforms, just before the change of the millennium. The government has focused on smaller and provincial or municipal state-owned enterprises (SOEs), sparing large, nation-wide enterprises with high visibility. The contribution of SOEs to overall GDP has steadily declined over the past 20 years, and interestingly, the remaining enterprises in 2017 register higher profits and net margins than their private-sector counterparts. Most likely, this is a result of the relative high industry concentration in which the remaining SOEs are competing. While the government has signalled a firm intention to privatize most of these large enterprises too, there are many important regulatory choices to be made. On the other hand, this particular group of large companies may represent an ideal vehicle for furthering a state-led industrialization. The indecisiveness of the government at the end of 2019 to push aggressively ahead signals that the state may still ponder about the idea to retain a force in the economy through these companies or "State Economic Groups". In parallel to the privatization process, the government has made efforts to strengthen the corporate governance regulations and legislations needed to protect ownership rights in listed companies, to increase transparency, to monitor top management in private companies, and generally to attract foreign investors. These regulations lag behind Asian peers and there is more action needed from both the private and public sectors to attain levels that reflects the ambitions of the government to increase the private sector.

Chapters 5–7 have focused more on the changes that have been brought to Vietnam by the political economic changes that have taken place over recent decades. Perhaps the most noticeable of such changes has been the spatial rearrangement of economic activities and the people who conduct them. The movement from agriculture to industry has seen people move to places of production in SEZs of various kinds and the emergence of infrastructure to link these with the places of consumption both within the domestic economy and overseas. While this process has brought about the lifting of the country from low to middle income status, it has also produced various negative externalities, which are most plainly seen in the pollution and environmental degradation covered in Chap. 7. Combined with the increasingly evident signs of global climate change, the challenges facing the country as a result of these effects is immense. At the very least, a rapid and large-scale switch to renewable energy and a commitment to good manufacturing practices across the country is necessary to avoid the situation becoming worse until credible, multilateral solutions are conceived and implemented.

This book began with an explanation, derived from Mill, of the range of issues to be considered in a work covering the political economy of a country and a suggestion of the questions that might be answered. It was then observed that the nature of the answers in the case of Vietnam would be affected by the time at which changes had come, which was a period significantly later than other East and Southeast Asian nations had passed through their periods of rapid industrialisation. In the case of Vietnam, change had come at a time of greatly enhanced international mobility, hence trade and then globalisation, in a rules-based international environment with one confirmed superpower and the possible rise of a second one. The process of economic development has extensively featured inwards FDI at a time when a wide range of business activities has become not just possible but inexpensive and convenient. It remains to be seen whether a new stage of development can be managed post labour cost competitiveness either by weathering the social and political pressures that would follow rebalancing of the economy by stimulating domestic demand or else through the removal of people from many activities that the coronavirus pandemic might bring.

Taken together, this book paints a mixed picture about the ambitions and successes during the reform period started in 1986. Choices that have shaped the political economy of Vietnam over the last 30 years have resulted in a reduced influence of the state and in increased prominence of markets. Vietnam exhibits a relatively prominent but inefficient state apparatus, with a relatively efficient but underregulated private sector. This tasks the government to be decisive in the future about the chosen vector to sustained economic growth.

Reference

Amsden AH (1989) Asia's next giant: South Korea and late industrialization. Oxford University Press, New York, NY

The manufacturer's authorised representative in the EU is Springer Nature Customer Service Centre GmbH, Europaplatz 3, 69115 Heidelberg, Germany. If you have any concerns regarding our products, please contact ProductSafety@springernature.com

Printed and bound by CPI Group (UK) Ltd, Croydon, CR0 4YY
30/09/2026
02225261-0011